GLOBAL SLOVAKIA
www.globalslovakia.com

Dedicated to the countless families who left the Old Country to chase their dreams across the ocean, and to the United States of America—a nation of now 250 years that will be forever shaped by the courage and sacrifice of these settlers.

ACROSS THE OCEAN

How Slovaks Settled in America

By Zuzana Palovic and
Gabriela Bereghazyova

Global Slovakia
Agátová 1323
905 01 Senica
Slovakia
www.globalslovakia.com

First published in 2026
Zuzana Palovic and Gabriela Bereghazyova assert their moral right to be identified as authors of this work.

Text © Zuzana Palovic and Gabriela Bereghazyova 2025
Artwork © Rebeka Jurcackova
Graphic design © Zuzana Chmelová
Editors: Margaret Bendet, Ken Duda, Jeanne Zulick
Historical consultant: Professor Michael Kopanic

ISBN 978-1-7374054-9-8

All rights are reserved. No part of this publication may be reproduced, stored in a retrieval system, or transmitted in any form or by any means, electronic, mechanical, photocopying, recording, or otherwise, without prior written permission of the publisher.

Table of contents

Foreword by Dan Hooks	7
Part I. **ROOTS IN THE OLD COUNTRY**	10
Part II. **TORN APART**	50
Part III. **REUNITED**	106
Part IV. **BACK TO ROOTS**	144
Afterword	180
Epilogue	183
Acknowledgments	186
Wall of Gratitude	187
About the Authors	188
About Global Slovakia	197
Our Partners	200

Authors' Note

This novel is a work of historical fiction, inspired by real events. While the backdrop is grounded in factual research, all of the characters in this story are fictional, and any resemblance to actual persons, living or dead, is purely coincidental.

The authors have taken care to ensure accuracy regarding the time period, locations, and events described. Some details, however, have been altered, condensed, or dramatized for narrative purposes.

FOREWORD

There is honor and pride to be found in surviving a good struggle—especially if you win.

This book took me on that journey my great grandfather took so long ago. It helped me feel, taste, and even smell the hardships he endured along the way. From the bottom of the ship to the grime and sweat of the coal mines and finally the smell of fresh hay and plowed soil from his field in what was then known as Slovaktown, Arkansas.

It brought memories of the "old people" I grew up around on an Arkansas family farm as the eldest of seven children.

I remember the one-room house my great grandmother spent her last years in and the smell of my Aunt Annie's kitchen with the wood stove. I was young, but I saw mules being used in the hay field and heard how many my grandfather owned before the first tractors were available. There was always a big garden, and there were canned vegetables and fruit of all kinds. We had apple, pear, plum, and pecan trees. We had cows for milk and meat. Except for the pecan trees, most of that is long gone.

My grandfather was born in Pennsylvania. Together with his parents, they were among the Slovaks who came to the Grand Prairie because of an abundance of land they would try to make their own.

They were farmers—not miners, steel workers, or anything else. They carved their fields from a rich prairie covered with very tall grass, and they built homes on the land. The nearest town was ten miles away. They didn't speak English, and there was no government office to offer assistance. They made a life where there had been none. They were tough. They worked, played, and prayed hard.

Not all who came stayed, but those who did stay left a legacy that continues to this day.

We celebrate that legacy with Slovak Heritage Day held in February as close as possible to the feast of Saints Cyril and Methodius. It's an important day because history fades if it's not studied and honored. Memories and stories disappear as the "story tellers" themselves become memories. On this day we come together to share family photos and memorabilia. We enjoy *pirohy, halušky, klobásy,* and *koláče* just like our grandparents and great-grandparents did.

Now I find myself being one of the "old people," trying to pass it all down and wanting to keep the history alive.

I have been fortunate to visit Slovakia twice, and each time brought unforgettable experiences. One of the most meaningful was visiting with cousins we found in my ancestors' village. It is difficult to put into words what it feels like to sit with family you never knew existed, speaking a language you don't understand, and yet realizing how much you have in common.

We met people and saw photographs of other people who resembled family and acquaintances back home in Arkansas. Despite the language barrier, there were lots of smiles, laughter, singing, and the kind of easy interactions that only family can have.

I learned that the men of my family are farmers, like me. Their daughter is a nurse, like my wife. Their son is a competitive shooter and hunter, also like me. An uncle proudly showed me his rifle, and together we drank *slivovica*. We almost didn't need a translator.

Others in our group had similar experiences. One young woman told us about meeting her family and shared that after dinner, the grandmother of the house offered her some coffee. When she declined, explaining she didn't drink coffee, the older woman loudly exclaimed, "We are related! No one in this family drinks coffee!" These types of encounters were repeated over and over again.

On the second trip with Zuzana and Gabriela of Global Slovakia, we were honored to visit the Presidential Palace in Bratislava and to be welcomed by (now former) President Čaputová herself. She was warm and gracious and acknowledged the common thread that connects us. She treated us as Slovaks. I remain deeply grateful for this meeting and cherish the memory.

My appreciation is stronger than ever for the Slovak families of Arkansas—my own included—and for the community they built and continue to maintain. There is honor and pride to be found in surviving a good struggle—especially if you win.

Slovaks everywhere can see themselves in this story. Any immigrant family can place their own name where "Sobota" stands and, through this book, relive a piece of their history.

Dan Hooks
Slovak, Arkansas
September 2025

PART 1
ROOTS IN THE OLD COUNTRY

In the Old Country
KRIVANY, SPRING 1894

The year was 1894, and the land of towering mountains and emerald valleys that Slovaks tenderly called *slovenská zem*[1] was still known merely as Upper Hungary.

Here, where the peaks of the Tatras pierced the clouds, people had for centuries lived peaceful, simple lives, guided by the rhythms of nature and the values of kinship. Their hearts were as deeply rooted in the land as the mighty lindens that dotted the hillsides.

One of these people was Juraj, a humble farmer from the village of Krivany.[2]

Our tale finds Juraj in the anticipation of an unfolding spring, tilling his narrow strip of rocky soil, his mind adrift and his forehead wrinkled with worry.

Teasing out a sustenance from the reluctant land is never a task for the fainthearted, and though Juraj was no stranger to hard work, the last two harvests had yielded little more than disappointment.

---

1 Slovak land
2 Krivany sits in the northeastern corner of the Šariš region in eastern Slovakia.

The nagging doubt in his heart was growing.

"Will the seeds sprout abundantly this year?" he wondered.

As ancient custom dictated, he mixed these seeds with blessed crumbs saved from last year's Christmas dinner—a rite believed to bestow the earth with fertility. Whether or not this was superstition, Juraj felt he needed all the help he could get.

For nine years, he had shared his life with Anna, their love growing stronger with each passing season. Together, they had welcomed their treasures: bright-eyed Jakub and, a year later, gentle Marienka.

In the eyes of the local village folk, the Sobotas were considered fortunate—one of the few families that always seemed to have enough. Perhaps it was the extra chickens in their coop or the children's rosy cheeks that gave this impression.

But Juraj and Anna knew the truth. For all their earnest effort, they could barely make ends meet.

There were times when food was scarce in their family, too.

In the dead of the night and away from their children's inquiring eyes, the parents prayed that their hard work and faith would see them through to a better tomorrow. Having survived two poor harvests, they knew a third would spell disaster.

But it was spring, and the air tingled with a promise of new beginnings. As skylarks serenaded the waking earth and snowdrops, dainty white flowers, emerged from the thawing ground, optimism stirred even in the weary souls of the village folk.

Before the first ray of sunrise touched the mountains, Juraj would rise from their shared bed. In the darkness, he wrapped a few slices of Anna's precious rye bread in a cloth and set out toward his field.

Plowing the stubborn patch of soil he owned, Juraj allowed himself to daydream of endlessly wide fields that would yield abundant harvests, and of a future where his children would never know hunger.

"One day," he vowed to himself and to God above, "I will buy more land and livestock and build a big, comfortable home where my family will thrive."

Little did he know, this spring he was sowing more than just rye. Hidden from plain sight, a dream had taken root deep within Juraj's heart.

As it began to bud, this dream nudged Juraj to work even harder, long after his blistered hands began to bleed and the sun dipped below the horizon. Only then would Juraj turn toward home, his tired feet quickening at the whiff of his wife's fresh bread carried forward by the evening breeze.

Inside their *drevenica*,[3] Anna had her hands full, readying the meal and baking bread for the week ahead, as she did every Saturday.

Her mother had taught her that making bread was a woman's sacred duty, where patience and prayer were as essential as flour and yeast.

---

3 Log cabin

Years of practice had taught her fingers to know when the dough was ready, had sharpened her instincts to sense when the oven was hot enough, had trained her ears to hear the subtle hollow sound of perfectly baked dough. When the loaves finally emerged, bronzed and fragrant, Anna blessed them with the sign of the cross.

The aroma beckoned Juraj to hurry home and also summoned their children; with hopeful eyes they followed Anna's every movement around the stone oven.

She smiled knowingly, for she had been such a child once, too. With a mother's wisdom, she always set aside a little dough to make small flatbreads just for them—clever strategy to protect the precious weekly loaves from her little "thieves."

As usual, they scoffed the treat down like hungry wolves, blissfully unaware of the family's shrinking reserves of grain.

With the children busy laying down wooden spoons on the sturdy oak table, Anna took a moment to scrutinize the tiny space. Juraj would return from the field soon, and she wanted him to rest in a cozy and tidy home.

It was the least she could do for her beloved husband, who was working harder than usual now.

Anna slid her gaze from the stove, where a stew of cabbage and potatoes was bubbling, to the bed, which they all shared in the corner of the dimly lit space. She quietly counted her blessings. At least they had a home they could call their own. Yes, it was just one room, and it was meager—but it was theirs.

Not everyone in the village was so lucky. Most of Anna's friends had moved into their husbands' family homes, where they lived with their in-laws and even their husbands' siblings. In the tight multigenerational quarters, it was not uncommon for petty squabbles to boil over into bitter arguments and long-held grudges.

When the familiar sound of Juraj's footsteps reached the threshold of their home, the day's hard toil seemed to melt from his face in the warmth of his family's love—even if only for a little while.

Around the old oak table, the Sobotas enjoyed more than just bread and stew—they shared stories, laughter, and the quiet joy of being together. The children's eager tales of their daily adventures entwined with their parents' relief of being able to provide shelter and a warm meal for their family.

"May it always be so," Anna whispered as she reached for Juraj's calloused hand across the worn tablecloth.

That evening, Anna watched the dying embers in their humble hearth, stroking the heads of her sleeping children and pondering what future God had planned for them.

She couldn't have known that destiny had already set its wheels in motion.

Seasons of Faith
SPRING & SUMMER 1894

That year, it rained on Good Friday. Village elders said that rain on this sacred day was a promise of a good harvest.

Juraj, like countless generations of farmers before him, watched the sky and read the signs in nature.

He believed that God wove messages into creation—subtle omens, meant for those who knew how to understand their meaning.

And the gentle drizzle that fell on Good Friday only affirmed that what he longed to believe with all his heart was true—Krivany and the Sobota family would be blessed with a bountiful crop this season.

All the more reason to celebrate Easter Sunday with everything they had. It would be another 274 days before the community would come together to rejoice so abundantly again.

As the holiest day in the Christian calendar dawned, the family dressed in their finest *kroje*,[4] each one hand-em-

---

4 Traditional folk costume

broidered with red and blue ornaments that had been passed down through generations.

Marienka stood still to let Anna adjust her ribbons, the child's usual restlessness tempered by the solemnity of the occasion. Even little Jakub seemed to sense the day's importance, standing proudly in the miniature version of his father's studded vest.

The Easter basket, the embodiment of the family's hopes and desires, waited by the front door, ready to be carried to the church. Anna arranged the basket with reverent precision, aware that each item of food carried a deeper meaning. The ham symbolized abundance; the hand-painted eggs, rebirth; the salt stood for health; and the special Easter bread was the emblem of the life-giving sun and the sacrifice of Jesus Christ.

Anna murmured a prayer as she draped the basket with a special cloth her grandmother had embroidered.

The church path, treaded by generations of faithful feet, wound past familiar gardens where wind-battered plum trees stretched their gnarly branches toward the sun.

Today, it seemed to Anna that she could feel every one of her ancestors walking beside them, as the family arrived at the whitewashed church in the village square.

Having laid the basket among dozens of others at the altar, Anna joined the other married women in their pews. The children eagerly took seats next to their friends in the front rows of the church, while Juraj stood proudly with the village men in the back of the hall.

Men, women, and children sat apart—just as they always had. It was their tradition, and they liked to honor it.

Surrounded by the strength of the community, the guidance of the sermon, and the sound of the organ reverberating throughout the hall, the congregation drew comfort from this annual ritual. Once again, it seemed that no obstacle was too great to overcome together.

The good people of Krivany could not have known that within a few short months, the potatoes they had planted with such love and care, would fall prey to a mysterious rot spreading across Europe.

Dear Reader, for now, let them bask in the spring sunshine and the celebration of their holy day.

Let them also look forward to the pleasures of a Slovak summer—to evenings filled with laughter, and to the comfort of falling asleep to the sound of crickets chirping in sweet-smelling haylofts. There would be time enough to worry later.

And, of course, the worries did come.

Following summer, as the growing season drew to an end, Juraj and Anna watched the sky with rising anxiety.

Would the weather hold for the autumn harvest? Last year's relentless rains had destroyed much of their rye, and now every passing cloud cast a dark shadow over their hearts and kept them awake through the balmy September nights.

When harvest time came, there was no moment to waste. Anna joined Juraj in the fields, and the two of them worked from dawn until dusk, their backs bent under the weight of the labor and their faces browned by the blazing sun. They gave their all—scything the rye and carefully tying it into bundles; digging the potatoes and carrots from the earth, one by one.

As the final wagon creaked its way to the barn, the grim reality could no longer be denied: it was another dismal harvest. The Sobota family's food supplies were dangerously low.

They had done everything right. They had followed every tradition, offered every prayer, worked every day until their muscles ached and hands bled—and still nature had withheld its bounty.

Was this a trial or a punishment from God?

Anna had learned how to be resourceful from her mother, a woman who had mastered the art of making a little go a long way. Although Anna's housewifely skills had served the Sobotas well, the hard times were proving that there is a limit to human creativity and human will as well.

The winter of 1894 set in early.

When the first frosts silvered the morning grass, Anna felt a familiar pang of fear as she surveyed the small amount of food stores she had: a small pile of potatoes, strings of dried mushrooms, and a precious few jars of fermented cabbage and beets. She knew that a lean winter lay ahead.

The cold, dark months seemed to stretch endlessly—broken only by the brief joy of Christmas, when ancient traditions rekindled a flicker of hope in the hearts of the community.

The Sobotas drew protective chalk circles around their cottage, swept their home's corners with a goose feather, and prayed fervently at the village church.

In times like these, a person couldn't be too careful, which is why everyone in the village embraced the old superstitions, in addition to their Christian prayers. When it came to protection, more was always better than none. After all, no one wanted to risk missing out on divine favor.

When Christmas Eve arrived, Marienka helped dress the table with the special cloth used only for the holiest of feasts, her small hands smoothing each wrinkle with great attention, just as her mother had taught her.

Fresh straw scattered beneath the table recalled the manger in Bethlehem, and the chain wrapped around the table legs would protect the family's togetherness.

As the first star rose in the night sky, everything was ready for the Christmas Eve feast.

This was more than a meal; it was a ritual to entice abundance and good fortune, both sorely needed after yet another trying year.

Juraj, standing at the head of the table, led the family in prayer. Then, Anna took a small clay jar of honey and marked the sign of the cross on each family member's forehead. "For sweetness in life," she whispered.

Then began their humble feast.

First came the *oblátky*, thin wafers lovingly prepared by the village teacher, and a mushroom soup made from treasured dried mushrooms the children had gathered in autumn. Then there were dried apples, golden *bobálky*—soft bread balls drizzled with honey and sprinkled with poppy seeds—and plump *pirohy*[5] stuffed with sauerkraut and potatoes.

---

5 Crescent-shaped dumplings

The contented sighs of the little ones offered brief relief from the ever-present worries weighing on their parents' hearts.

But once the children were tucked into bed and the house fell quiet, Juraj and Anna's thoughts drifted once more to the family's uncertain future. They knew they couldn't survive another winter following on a failed harvest. Something would have to change.

May God have mercy on them...

What Will Become of Us?
FEBRUARY 1895

The winter wind howled through the roof of the Sobota's *drevenica* as Juraj and Anna counted their modest savings by candlelight.

Anna's delicate embroidery and Juraj's intricate ood carvings brought in a little extra income at the local market during the long months when the land slumbered beneath a thick blanket of snow.

But despite their best efforts, the family remained trapped in a relentless cycle of poverty—always seeming to be just a penny away from starvation.

No matter how hard Anna and Juraj worked or how masterfully they applied their crafts, they were denied the fertile field of their dreams and the better life they believed it would offer.

Perhaps the children could fare better.

But for that, they knew, their children would need to go to school.

In the late 1800s, Slovak families like the Sobotas faced an impossible conundrum. As much as Juraj and Anna wanted their children to attend school, they had no choice but to play the cards they had been dealt. The family's existence depended on every pair of hands helping around the farm, and that included the children.

Jakub and Marienka could go to school consistently only in winter, and even then, the path to learning was fraught with obstacles. In winter, the twenty-minute walk to the schoolhouse was transformed into a treacherous journey through the knee-deep snow.

Their poor harvests left the Sobotas unable to afford more than one pair of shoes for their children. This meant that the brother and sister had to share a pair of worn leather boots—and take turns attending classes.

On her days at school, Marienka would stuff the boots with an extra pair of woolen socks, her tiny feet swimming in the heavy brown leather that seemed to laugh at every clumsy step she took forward.

Truth be told, the children were relieved when they didn't have to go.

Their teacher's only language was Hungarian, and he treated the children's native Slovak tongue as if speaking it were a crime. Why?

Dear Reader, this was a time when the Kingdom of Hungary was aggressively promoting Magyarization, an ambitious policy designed to transform the country's diverse peoples into a single Hungarian nation.

Kubko[6] endured endless humiliation for his struggles to learn Hungarian, and Marienka could not understand

---

6 A diminutive of Jakub

why she was not allowed to speak with her classmates in the language they all spoke at home, and everywhere else.

Was it any wonder that the children found more joy and peace tending to their small farm?

The family's cheerful flock of chickens, three mischievous goats, two burly sheep, and one playful little piglet provided them with not just the essential milk, cheese, wool, and meat, but also friendship, fun, and learning.

What was the point of being stuck in a classroom all day anyway?

Life in Šariš County followed a predictable rhythm, rooted in tradition but offering few opportunities beyond agriculture.

The local ceramic workshop and textile mill were too small to employ everyone, leaving most families to scrape out a living from increasingly insufficient, narrow strips of inherited farmland.

Jakub would most likely grow up to be a farmer, just like his father. Marienka would take on the role of a wife and mother, as was expected of all women.

At the tender age of eight, Jakub was already joining his father in the fields, learning the ancient wisdom of farming like a devoted apprentice. Each task he was given was more than a chore. It was a lesson in becoming a farmer—and, in the eyes of his community, becoming a man.

Under his father's instruction, Jakub learned to read the sky for weather and to feel the soil's readiness between his fingers. Making and mending farm equipment became lessons in patience and resourcefulness, virtues that would serve him well as a provider for his own wife and family.

In the same way, Marienka, bright-eyed and eager, studied under her mother's gentle guidance, learning the art of being a homemaker.

Each dawn, Marienka would follow her mother to milk the goats and gather the fresh eggs from beneath the drowsy hens. Again, these weren't mere chores; they were preparations for her future role at the heart of her own family.

The skills Marienka learned now—from managing a larder to turning humble ingredients into nourishing meals—would one day contribute to deciding her worth as a bride.

Life in Krivany might have continued flowing as it had always done, but fate had different plans for the Sobotas.

Great journeys are sometimes launched by small events, and—in Juraj's case—the journey began from a string of perfectly smoked *klobása*.[7]

But, dear Reader, let us first look at what was happening on the other side of the world, far away from little Slovakia.

---

7 Sausage

Meanwhile in America

1890s

Across the ocean, in the United States of America, the mighty engine of the Industrial Revolution roared with ferocity, devouring everything in its path.

New factories sprang forth one by one, like mushrooms after rain. Railroad tracks crisscrossed the country, connecting the coasts of this great continent and all points in between. Overnight, cities sprouted where nothing but wilderness had stood before.

The miracle of progress came at a terrible price.

Beneath the surface, coal mines dug deeper and deeper into the darkness. Above ground, steel mills blazed with what seemed to be an eternal fire. The once clear air grew thick with black soot, and the crystal blue streams turned murky grey from all the waste. Industrial America was thundering day and night, and it had an insatiable hunger for workers.

The Irish were first to answer the call. They worked hard, only to find their dreams of prosperity shattered by sixteen-hour workdays, starvation wages, and employment conditions that broke both body and spirit.

Coffins filled with bodies that had fallen victim to the dangerous working conditions, and so the Irish began to unite. Their demands were simple. If they were to continue working, they wanted situations resonant with basic human dignity: fair pay, safer conditions, and shorter hours.

The captains of industry regarded these ultimatums with cold disdain.

Raising wages and improving safety compromised their company's profits. In their marble-floored offices, far from the heat and grime of the factories, these titans of industry found a simple solution: if the Irish refused to bend, they would find workers who would.

For their newest source of manpower, the mill and mine owners turned their gaze eastward, toward Slavic Europe.

The Slavs embodied everything the industrialists desired: good health, strong bodies, and temperaments shaped by centuries of feudal hardship. They were perfect workers, willing to take on the most dangerous jobs for the very wages the Irish had said were unlivable.

But even the most desperate man wouldn't abandon his homeland without persuasion. And so, the industrial barons unleashed their secret weapon: silver-tongued dream weavers.

These agents—polished, worldly men trained in the art of psychological seduction—were dispatched to Eastern Europe with a single mission: to paint America in colors so brilliant they would blind their audience to reality.

With beating drums and blaring trumpets, the agents paraded into the most remote villages of the Kingdom of

Hungary. Dressed in sleek suits and flashing thick gold watch chains that glinted in the sun, these representatives of industry stood before the villagers with an air of unshakable confidence.

They were walking advertisements of American success.

Standing in village squares, leather briefcases in hand, these cosmopolitan showmen spun dazzling tales of prosperity and abundance.

They spoke of a benevolent American emperor who pleaded for help, inviting the downtrodden Slavs to come to America, where gold nuggets rolled down the streets.

And so, village by village, the local men began to pack their bags.

The American Emperor Calls
LATE FEBRUARY 1895

On a bitterly cold February evening in 1895, Juraj was delivering sausages to the local inn—just one of the many ways the Sobotas used their skills to stretch their meager income.

His family's secret sausage recipe, passed down from father to son over generations, had earned Juraj a well-deserved reputation throughout Krivany. The Jewish innkeeper prized Juraj's smoked delicacy highly, knowing that its rich flavor enticed his patrons to order more rounds of his home-brewed *slivovica*.[8] Paired with fresh bread and a crisp slice of onion, the sausage was the tastiest of all the local foods.

As Juraj entered the dimly lit tavern quarters on that day, something stirred in his soul. He found himself inexplicably drawn to a peculiar figure.

The stranger presented an imposing sight. With every sweeping gesture, his suit jacket shifted, and the chain

---

8 Plum brandy

of a gleaming gold pocket watch flashed in the glow of the oil lamps. When he took a step, coins jingled in his pockets.

The man spoke in a booming voice, spinning tales of buildings made of towering glass that reached the heavens.

His audience, a crowd of weather-hardened farmers, leaned forward in their seats, and those standing at the rear of the crowded room stretched their necks so they could get a good look at this compelling stranger.

That night, they got drunk not on their usual plum brandy but a dazzling tale of an American emperor and his streets lined with gold.

Juraj studied the man's fine wool blazer, iron-pressed shirt, and shiny black leather boots. "Surely," he thought, "a man who has found such success in life would have no reason to lie?"

When the stranger produced photographs of impossible-to-imagine cities, Juraj stared at the forests of glass and steel buildings in disbelief.

In that moment, the fairytale began to feel like an opportunity.

Could this *Amerika* be the answer to his prayers?

Like his ancestors before him, Juraj's world had been bound by the lush green hills that circled his village. For generations, the Sobotas lineage had lived and died within sight of the same church tower.

During those times, it was rare for anyone to move away from their native village, let alone from their county and kingdom. The bond to family, tradition, and land was strong in this part of the world.

But it was also the legacy of feudalism that had shackled Slovak farmers to the land.

Through the Middle Ages, the labor system confined peasants to the soil they were born on. There, they would live, work, and die, tilling the land they didn't even own.

Dear Reader, feudalism bestowed immense power on the few over the many. It was an era when kings were believed to be endowed by God with the right to own all the land and make all the decisions.

Still, no ruler could control the vast stretches of the kingdom alone. To maintain order, the monarch granted lofty titles, expansive estates, and the power to wield great influence over this land to his trusted inner circle.

The mighty lords, in turn, needed workers to tend to their fields and manage their estates.

This was long before anyone heard of human rights and fair wages. The common folk were property tied to the land and to their landlords. A benevolent lord might allow his peasants to prosper, but a cruel one could sentence generations into poverty and destitution with a wave of his hand.

Juraj's grandparents couldn't simply leave their village in search of better opportunities elsewhere, but Juraj was born into a different world.

Nearly fifty years ago, a revolution rocked the Kingdom of Hungary and changed everything.

In 1848, peasants were granted basic civil liberties, forever breaking the chains of serfdom. For the first time in history, people like Juraj were able to chart their own destinies, an idea that had once been unthinkable.

Yet, the political change could not magically wipe out poverty from the Slovak countryside, and freedom without resources is like a plow without a field.

When the American emperor came knocking, Slovaks listened.

What started as a trickle of the most adventurous and desperate soon swelled into a flood, with hundreds of thousands of Slovaks setting sail for distant shores every year in search of fortune.

An American fever had taken hold over *slovenská zem*, burning away centuries of tradition with the promise of wealth.

Where There's a Will, There's a Way
SPRING 1895

Slovak women, entrusted with the duty of keeping families together for centuries, were not so easily persuaded.

Anna met with skepticism the golden promises Juraj had heard at the local inn.

Rural life revolved around family. Everything depended on family togetherness. Family softened life's blows, and family was the source of one's joy. It was impossible to imagine being apart.

But Juraj painted their future in bright colors. He spoke of having fields of their own land that would burst with potatoes and lush cabbage, orchards heavy with sweet apples. He promised Anna fine wheat flour instead of rough rye. Delicate fabrics to replace homespun wool. Not just one cow but two. A wealth beyond their wildest dreams.

They would never again go to bed hungry.

With each passing day, Anna's objections melted away like the winter snow around them. An American dream began to take root in her heart as well—not of a life in which the streets were paved with gold but a life where her children's bellies would be full and where winter wouldn't be a season of fear.

At last, she understood that America was an opportunity, it was also a sacrifice. Reluctantly, she gave her silent blessing to Juraj.

But the path ahead proved far thornier than the silver-tongued agent had said it would be.

To begin with, the cheapest ticket on the steamship cost more than the Sobotas could imagine earning in the next several years.

There was no America without a steamship ticket, so Juraj and Anna turned to family first, then their friends, but found only empty pockets and apologetic smiles. No one had much to give:

Again and again, they heard, "*Sami nemáme.*"9

With heavy hearts, husband and wife resolved to sell off most of their farm animals, keeping only the chickens and a goat so that Anna and the children would have enough to eat while Juraj was gone.

Still, they were luckier than most.

Across the kingdom, other families were selling ancestral homes and fields in order to secure a steerage ticket. Worse still, vultures operating in the murky waters of transatlantic travel sat ready to prey on the desperate. Smooth-talking men in city clothes sold fake tickets and forged papers. Their victims discovered the truth only when it was too late.

---

9 We don't have enough, ourselves.

The passport, though, proved a more formidable obstacle than money.

In the Austria-Hungary of the 1890s, the travel document we take for granted today was a privilege, not a right.

Tensions were simmering across the continent and young men were fleeing in droves, and in response the authorities had grown strict. If all the able-bodied men were in America, who would fight the country's wars? After all, there is no empire without an army.

A new obstacle was introduced to keep males at home—travel permits to leave the Kingdom became mandatory. Getting such a permit required more than determination; it took money, patience, perseverance... and bribes.

Like most people in Upper Hungary, Juraj and Anna could neither read nor write Slovak, and they couldn't speak Hungarian either. This left them at the mercy of the authorities, who showed no compassion for their plight.

Each of Juraj's encounters with a sneering Hungarian-speaking official ended in humiliation and rejection.

When the notification that Juraj's travel permit had been denied finally arrived, it shouldn't have come as a surprise. Yet, the news felt like a devastating blow to the Sobotas. They had already sacrificed so much.

Cattle Passport and Prayers

AUTUMN 1895

Two seasons passed after the American at the inn seduced Juraj to follow his sweet call, and still the Slovak seemed no closer to reaching his goal.

Was the dream to be finished before it had even started? Had he failed both as a husband and a father?

Necessity is the mother of invention, and with the legal paths closed to him, Juraj ventured into the shadows to find a solution.

This was a realm that existed in the back rooms of taverns and in whispered conversations behind the village church.

The grey zone teamed with men who made their living evading the empire's iron laws. These men "knew" men who could make papers appear out of thin air and make borders dissolve—for a price.

Here, promises were as easily made as they were risky to follow, as the price for failure was painfully high.

Could Juraj trust the word of a local crook who promised to smuggle him across the border? Or would the sly man pocket the family's last three gold coins and forget all about their agreement?

Juraj was about to lose his last ounce of hope when he heard a knock on his door. To his and Anna's great relief, it was the scar-faced smuggler, with a smirk on his face and a cattle passport in his hand.

Since neither Juraj nor Anna could read, they didn't realize that this was a passport intended for an animal and was unlikely to get Juraj safely across the border into Germany. The official-looking document filled them with optimism.

They knew that time was running out.

It was already late autumn. Soon, snow and ice would seal the mountain passes, making travel out of eastern Slovakia close to impossible. If he were to make it to America, Juraj would have to leave before the first snowfall.

The rush became a blessing in disguise.

Juraj threw himself into preparations—harvesting the last of the potatoes, patching up the roof that would shelter his family through winter, cutting enough firewood to last them until spring. During the day, being busy with work kept darker thoughts at bay.

But at night, lying beside his beloved Anna, doubt gnawed at him.

Who would protect the family while he chased promises across the ocean? What would happen to Anna and the children if, God forbid, he did not make it back from America? Every glance at them, vulnerable without him, made him question his resolve to depart.

Only a friend's solemn oath brought Juraj any peace. "I'll guard them with my life," the man had sworn, pressing his hand to his heart. "As if they were my own."

Journey into the Unknown
LATE OCTOBER 1895

Dawn broke on Juraj's twenty-eighth birthday, a day that would split his life in two.

With a heavy heart, he packed his humble belongings—his father's Bible, worn smooth at the corners from years of devotion; fresh bread, smoked cheese, and bacon prepared by Anna; and his finest *kroj,* which his mother had finished stitching just before death claimed her.

Juraj carefully wrapped everything in a rough hemp cloth and flung it over his shoulder.

As he stepped into the chilly morning air, his eye fell on the plump red rosehips smiling at him from a wild rose bush that grew near their cottage gate. How many times last year had he plucked those soft fruits, bringing them home to Anna after a long day in the fields? Would he ever again see this bush bloom and come to fruit?

As Juraj looked around the village of Krivany, tears silently streamed down his face. He wanted to seal every detail in his memory—the way the morning mist clung to the valley, the smell of woodsmoke from the chimneys, the soft ringing of the church bells.

Trees started to shed leaves—an unmistakable sign that winter was not far and a reminder that Juraj was leaving his family during the most challenging time of the year. Would Anna manage without him?

It was too late to change his mind.

Pushing back hot tears, Juraj bid farewell to his beautiful wife and two children.

Neighbors emerged from their homes to say their goodbyes, encircling the young man. Women wiped their eyes with aprons, men offered pats on the back. To them, Juraj was more than a farmer leaving his village—he was a hero bound for *Amerika*, carrying their own hopes and desires on his shoulders.

Behind the crowd, a hunched-over figure approached slowly.

It was Juraj's father.

The sight drained the blood from Juraj's face, and a wave of sadness rose inside him, threatening to overwhelm our hero. Juraj was the old man's only surviving son—his eldest boy perished from cholera some twenty years earlier, and the youngest one died together with his mother during childbirth.

Juraj was all that remained of his father's family, and now he, too, would be gone. The old man would never recover from the loss, and just one month after Juraj departed from Krivany, he too left—but for eternity.

Yet, on that fateful late October morning, he knew his son's happiness outweighed the pain of his own loss. He straightened the back bent by decades of heavy work, gazed up at Juraj, and pressed into his hand a bottle of his best *slivovica*.

No words were needed as the two men looked deeply into each other's eyes. The father understood his son, and the son thanked his father for the silent blessing.

Before climbing into a waiting wagon, Juraj paused, knelt down, and scooped up a bit of the dark soil that had nourished his family for generations. He wrapped it carefully in a handkerchief his wife had embroidered for him and tucked it safely into the pocket, close to his heart.

Little did he know then that this cherished little piece of Slovakia would bring him great comfort and solace in the months and years to come.

He was officially bound for America.

Although he couldn't know then how far away this goal on the other side of the ocean truly lay. Like most in his village, Juraj had never seen a map of the world. It was not that long ago that Slovaks thought America was just a hop, skip, and jump beyond the majestic Tatra Mountains. Though better informed now, Juraj had never before left the district of his home village, and he could not comprehend the distance of this voyage he was embarking on.

The short carriage ride brought the travelers to the edge of the imposing mountain wall. From this point forward, they would have to continue their journey on foot through the dense Carpathian pine forests. The thick canopy would provide cover from the hawkish eyes of the patrolling border guards.

Exposed roads were not safe for the band of illegal emigrants who carried a weight much heavier than that of

their forged passports. By leaving the kingdom without valid travel permits, the men were committing a serious crime—avoiding military service for the younger ones and shirking the reservist's responsibilities for older men like Juraj.

Nature, too, presented challenges to Juraj and his fellow travelers.

Heavy rain and biting winds extended the two-day journey to a treacherous week of slogging through the mud. To avoid being discovered, the smuggler forbade the band of illegal emigrants from starting a fire, and so the only solace was the occasional dry patch of land in a cave along the way.

When the men finally emerged at the train station in Sucha, on the frontier end of the Austro-Hungarian Empire, they were on the brink of exhaustion and nervous beyond words. After all, they were defying their duty to the crown, and discovery would mean prison—or worse.

The smuggler, practiced in such matters, moved with swift efficiency, not leaving anything to chance. He ushered the men toward an officer loitering at the end of the platform—and then discreetly slipped an envelope into the pocket of the officer's navy-blue uniform. The young Pole intentionally looked the other way, and the smuggler hissed an order for Juraj and the others to climb into the carriage.

Moments later, they were huddled in a train car, hearts pounding as its wheels set into motion with a puff of white smoke. Only then did they dare to breathe a sigh of relief.

They had made it! They were going to *Amerika*!

Taking swigs of *slivovica*, the men passed the time playing cards and sharing stories.

The fiery plum brandy burned away their fears and steadied their nerves as the train kept chugging. But even so, their eyes still darted to the windows at every stop, and conversations fell to mere whispers whenever footsteps passed their compartment.

To their dismay, the train did not deliver them to the port.

Germany had been plagued by cholera outbreaks for over a decade and had grown suspicious of migrants from Austria-Hungary. Who knew what contagious diseases these Slavs were bringing?

Just short of the German border, a sinister-looking man with a toothless smile emerged at the door of their cabin, rushing them out onto a nameless station. Once again, the travelers had to skulk through forests like thieves until instructed to board a train that would take them to their final destination. The international network of smugglers was surprisingly well-coordinated.

In the Port
BREMEN, NOVEMBER 1895

The train came to a screeching halt in Bremerhaven in Germany. Juraj stumbled onto the platform, his legs stiff from the long journey, and what he saw stole his breath away.

Ships of all sizes were moored along the harbor, and an enormous crowd of people from every corner of Europe stood on the wooden docks waiting to board.

Men, women, and children dressed in clothing he had never seen before, speaking languages he had never before heard, thronged around him. Street vendors barked their offers in a half a dozen tongues. Some held up sausages and bread to the hungry travelers; others offered completely unnecessary "equipment" for the voyage, such as tin dinnerware sets. Women in headscarves clutched children to their skirts, while men haggled over last-minute supplies.

Beyond the crowd, the SS *Trave* awaited, dominating the harbor like a floating castle. Juraj had never seen any structure so large as that ship.

Fresh paint gleamed on her hull, and her two chimneys and four masts reached toward the clouds. This boat would carry some thirteen hundred Europeans, including Juraj and his fellow Slovak travelers, to the port of New York City.

As glorious as this streamliner was, it was the power of that ocean that brought Juraj to his knees.

First, he tasted its salty air on his tongue and felt its sting in his eyes, and then he caught sight of the endless expanse of dark blue water glistening in the late afternoon sun.

"The enormity of the sea makes the grand ship look like a mere toy," Juraj thought.

Seeing the fragility of the ship and knowing that it was his destiny to board it made his heart pound wildly. Was he frightened of the unknown? Perhaps. But the excitement of the journey ahead far outweighed his momentary fear.

And there was no time to indulge or scrutinize his reactions.

The crew, shouting orders in an unfamiliar language, was already herding the steerage passengers into the belly of the ship.

When the massive engines roared, the harbor—and with it the old world—began to slip away. Juraj knew that life would never again be the same.

So, the epic ten-day ocean voyage began.

◆ ◆ ◆ ◆ ◆

PART 2

TORN APART

Across the Ocean
SS TRAVE, NOVEMBER 1895

Deep in steerage class, where a thousand souls were packed together like sardines, Juraj could barely distinguish day from night. It seemed to him that in the damp bowels of SS *Trave*, even time began to rot.

The young man's hands, calloused from years of working the soil, now lay useless in his lap. Never in his life had he known such nothingness. Ever since he was old enough to hold a rake, his days had been filled with work and purpose.

Enforced idleness brewed restlessness among the frustrated men.

In the cramped quarters, tempers flared over the smallest things—a misplaced elbow, a snore too loud, a glance held too long.

Juraj watched as the tame farmers and craftsmen turned into brawlers after a few shots of brandy. There was not a day that went by that he didn't have to dodge the curses and fists that were flying around. He learned quickly how to recognize the subtle shift in the atmosphere before steerage turned into a cauldron of squabbles. When a scuffle was about to break out, Juraj would move like a fox to find a sliver of solitude.

Getting into a fight was the last thing he needed.

Afloat on the Atlantic Ocean, the only signposts of time moving forward were the mealtimes when the hungry and grumpy men lined up for their fill of boiled meat, fish, or liver. Though plentiful, the food rarely inspired joy. The meat was tough, and the mysterious vegetable mash was best left untouched.

Potatoes, soup, and white bread were a safe bet, but Juraj's saving grace was the carefully rationed *slanina*[10] he'd brought from home. Each evening, he sliced a piece as thin as a sheet of paper, letting the bacon melt on his tongue.

In those special moments, the rich, smoky flavor transported him right back to Krivany and to the smokehouse where he'd prepared the bacon months ago, not knowing that it would accompany him on his journey to the other side of the world.

Just as Juraj was settling into the strange rhythm aboard the transatlantic liner, a storm struck. Even rats began to look for shelter when the ship rocked, rolled, and slammed down on the angry waves.

The well-trained crew hurried to close the hatches on the upper deck to prevent seawater from flooding into the boat. But when the heavy iron doors clanged shut, they trapped the steerage passengers below, cutting them off

---

10 Smoked cured pork belly

not only from fresh air, but also the precious few toilets on the upper deck.

In these trying hours, the sick relied on buckets that inevitably overflowed, their contents sloshing across the floor with each violent roll of the ship. The stench became unbearable, but even worse was the primal fear that Juraj felt in his stomach.

One wave after another battered the ship, and the only thing that he could do was pray that the boat would not sink into the cold, black depths of the ocean that night.

"Who knows how many unfortunate souls found their end in that void?" Juraj pondered, trying his best not to let the fear take over his thoughts.

The storm finally passed, the sky cleared, and the ocean calmed. Then the pale and weary steerage passengers emerged onto the upper deck to refresh themselves. Like a child discovering the world around him, Juraj, too, crawled out of the stifling third class.

Standing at the railing, gulping the clean air like a drowning man who's finally reached the water's surface, he witnessed something extraordinary—a magnificent sea creature appeared beside the ship.

Juraj gasped at the massive form rising gracefully from the impenetrable abyss. The creature's eye, ancient and knowing, seemed to look into his own before it released a spray of mist and sound that echoed deep into his bones. Later, Juraj learned that this gentle giant was called a whale and was a mammal just like himself.

Looking around, Juraj marveled at the mosaic of humanity that surrounded him. A thousand faces from every corner of Europe, each carrying their own dreams across the ocean.

Sometimes, in the evenings, a fellow passenger would produce a battered accordion or violin, and the entire steerage would come alive with song and dance. Polish *polka* mixed with Hungarian *csárdás* and Slovak *odzemok*,[11] until it seemed they were no longer separate peoples but a single tribe, united in their journey toward hope.

Then, on one cool morning, Juraj saw her, the Statue of Liberty, emerging from the mist like a vision from heaven.

His eyes widened in awe as the copper goddess rose before him, solemn and shining in the pale light. For a moment, time seemed to stand still.

"This is no dream... America is real," Juraj whispered to himself, over and over, as if the words alone could anchor him in this new world.

To the young man, she bore an uncanny resemblance to the Holy Mother, whose guidance he'd sought since childhood in the small church of his native village. Dropping to his knees, he began to pray *Zdravas Mária*,[12] thanking the heavens and his ancestors for helping him make it safely across the ocean.

In 1903, eight years after Juraj's journey, these apt and now-immortal words were inscribed on the pedestal of the Statue of Liberty:

---

11 A Slovak solo traditional dance for men.
12 Hail Mary

> Give me your tired, your poor,
> Your huddled masses yearning to breathe free,
> The wretched refuse of your teeming shore.
> Send these, the homeless, tempest-tost to me,
> I lift my lamp beside the golden door!

Seeing Liberty, holding aloft her beacon, Juraj and his fellow passengers wiped away tears and embraced one another, understanding that they had arrived at the threshold of their new lives.

Welcome to America

NEW YORK, NOVEMBER 1895

The SS *Trave* glided into the calm waters of New York Harbor and slowly docked at Ellis Island. An excited commotion took hold of the ship.

Passengers stretched their necks for a better view, marveling at the rows of buildings that reached into the clouds and seemed to stretch beyond them.

Throughout his journey, Juraj had encountered strange animals, unfamiliar people, and a whirlwind of new sights, sounds, and smells that surprised, shocked, and bewildered him. But none of this compared to the awe-striking sight that now unfolded before him: the towering Manhattan skyline—majestic, impossible, and utterly unlike anything he had ever imagined.

The dream was within reach, but he was not there yet.

Ellis Island: the two little words thickened the air on the cramped deck where the clustered immigrants stood shoulder to shoulder beneath the iron sky. The name made Juraj's blood run cold.

He had heard of heartbreaking stories about families torn apart by the strict American immigration controls. Such tales had earned Ellis Island the foreboding nickname "the Island of Tears." Juraj took a long, deep breath as he touched the fine handkerchief in his pocket and felt the familiar packet of soil from his village.

He was a strong, young man. "Surely, I have nothing to fear," he told himself. "I didn't come all this way to be stopped here." Yet his stomach twisted with dread when he entered the large immigration depot.

Dear Reader, Ellis Island was the country's busiest entry point. At its peak, this immigration center received two thousand souls a day.

Juraj and his fellow passengers aboard the SS *Trave* in the autumn of 1895 were but a single drop in a vast ocean of immigrants who arrived in the United States at the turn of the 19th and 20th centuries.

Inside this huge immigration station, the glum-faced U.S. officials moved with mechanical efficiency, largely indifferent to the terrors and tears of the newcomers. To the immigration officers, the people they processed were just batches of desperate foreigners who hoped to find riches in this country. They spoke little or no English. They were unkempt and unbathed. Why waste time or sympathy on them?

First came the medical exam. They called it the "six-second physical," and the name was no exaggeration. How else could doctors examine thousands of passengers every day?

Still, those six seconds stretched on like hours as the doctor's eyes scraped over Juraj, searching for any sign of illness or disease. A cry of despair pierced the air—another immigrant condemned to the holding pens on the other side of the hall, destined for the next ship back to Europe.

Unnerving as the medical exam might be, the task of the immigration officers was not to turn people away. It was to allow as many immigrants into the United States as possible. America needed every pair of hands to fuel the golden age of its Industrial Revolution. Men in the prime of their youth, like Juraj, were the kind of workforce the country needed.

After Juraj passed the medical exam, then came the questions—twenty-nine of them, fired like bullets from a stern immigration officer.

"Where are you from?"

"Do you have any money?"

"Can you read?"

"Do you have work lined up?"

Imagine how confused Juraj must have been when he was bombarded with questions about his health, wealth, and identity in a language he couldn't understand.

Juraj willed his hands to stop shaking, as he repeated the answers his fellow steerage passengers had taught him. Even he was surprised how confidently he stated, "Slovak" when asked about his origin.

The officer's pen scratched across the paper, and each stroke seemed like an eternity.

Finally, he looked up, smiled at the young immigrant, and exclaimed:

"Welcome to America, son!"

Juraj was overcome by relief. Joy surged through his veins, making him forget the tribulations of the journey and his tiredness.

This was his dream manifest, the culmination of nearly three years of planning, praying, saving, selling, hoping, and worrying.

In a daze, Juraj gathered his meager belongings and reached for his most precious possession: the *kroj* that his mother had lovingly crafted. Every stitch was imbued with a prayer for his future.

Juraj could feel his dignity and strength return as he fastened its many buttons, ribbons, and sturdy belt.

This was one of the grandest occasions of his entire life.

The young man had left little Krivany, crossed the enormous ocean, and now stood at the precipice of the gate of America. Every cell in Juraj's body reverberated with anticipation and satisfaction.

Dressed like a proud Slovak, he was ready to meet his new homeland.

But the moment Juraj stepped onto the streets of New York, curious glances quickly turned to sneers. Children pointed at him, and adults whispered as he walked past.

At first, Juraj thought the onlookers were admiring his native *kroj*. Clearly, they had never seen anything so beautiful before! But soon, the sweet triumph soured. What he had initially mistaken for admiration was in reality, judgment, and contempt. And this he knew soon enough.

The confused man thought, "How could this be?" He tried not to pay heed to the stares. He had no notion that his colorful handsewn outfit, full of love and history, appeared strange and foreign—even intimidating—to the locals.

It was not very long before Juraj's arrival that a group of *kroj*-clad Slovaks, walking from New York to the factories of New Jersey, had been chased out of a U.S. town with rocks and bullets. The Americans had confused this vibrant Slovak attire with the ceremonial costumes of Native Americans, and they feared these people were local aboriginals who had come to reclaim their stolen land.

Though no stones flew his way, each mocking laugh and suspicious glare struck deeper than any physical blow.

Downcast as he was, Juraj wasted no time feeling sorry for himself. He straightened his back and squared his shoulders. Let them stare. Let them laugh.

He hadn't come to America to make friends; he had come to make money.

Strangers to Brothers
USA, NOVEMBER 1895

With his pockets nearly empty and the factories of Pittsburgh still hundreds of miles away, Juraj joined a group of Slavic men making their way to Pennsylvania on foot.

Their guide was a seasoned Polish migrant who had made the journey more than once before and who seemed to know every shortcut and safe resting spot.

For more than a week, the seventeen men marched along the winding railroad tracks, on dusty country roads, and even along the trails of the rugged Appalachian Mountains.

A camaraderie born from their shared strife eased the anxiety they carried within. With each mile they walked together, the group slowly transformed—from men tossed together by fate into something closer to a brotherhood. Though they spoke in a babel of Slavic tongues—Slovak, Polish, Rusyn, Ukrainian—their language of hope and determination needed no translation.

When night fell, they made camp beneath star-studded skies, the flicker of their fires piercing the vast darkness that surrounded them.

In those quiet hours, they understood one thing clearly: they were stronger together than any one of them was on his own. And so, they shared what little they had—hard bread pulled from worn packs, small game or rodents caught along the trail, and precious sips of home-distilled spirits that burned with the taste of the villages they had left behind.

When Juraj's harmonica sang into the night, its aching melodies carried their hearts back across the ocean to their loved ones. One day, they would return.

November 1895 blessed them with unusual warmth, but the mountain trails showed no mercy to their boots.

One by one, their shoes surrendered to the endless walking, leaving a trail of broken leather like breadcrumbs through the wilderness. By the journey's end, most trudged onward with feet wrapped in rags.

Among these travelers, Juraj found not just a companion, but a kindred spirit in Michal, a Rusyn from Čirč.

The two men's home villages lay so close that they might have passed each other a hundred times before at market days or foraging in the mushroom-rich forests back home.

In any event, here they were now, walking side by side in this strange new world.

Juraj and Michal shared stories of their past lives and whispered dreams of success in America. Around the fire one night, Michal spoke of contacts he knew in the Duquesne mines and invited Juraj to join him. There was more than enough work to go around in the Pittsburgh coal industry, he promised, and he was certain Juraj could land a job there.

Juraj welcomed the offer—it was the only glimpse of solid ground in an otherwise uncertain time.

On their final evening together, gathered around a campfire on the brink of the city, the seventeen men sat in contemplative silence. Their destination was within reach. Tomorrow would mark the start of a new chapter in their American story.

As Juraj and Michal shook hands over the dying embers, making a pact to look out for one another, they could not have known that their lives and destinies would be intertwined forever.

Streets of Gold and Buckets of Coal

USA, NOVEMBER 1895

The weary group came to a halt on the foggy outskirts of Pittsburgh, staring in disbelief at the sprawling city that stretched out before them.

Tall chimneys pierced the sky, belching thick black smoke that blanketed everything in a dull, ashen haze.

The roar of industry, the hiss of steam, the shriek of factory whistles, the grinding pulse of machinery, created an otherworldly symphony that filled Juraj not with wonder but with a growing sense of dread.

Each breath burned with ash and coal dust, and Juraj's eyes watered as he surveyed row upon row of narrow, two-story houses crammed together, their rooftops and windows covered in black dust.

Where were the streets lined with gold he had been promised?

But, Dear Reader, it was not the soot-filled skies or the gloomy factory buildings that most frightened these immigrants. What sent a cold chill of terror down their spines were the men they saw shuffling along the street.

The shells of men wandering the streets of Pittsburgh were far from the picture of prosperity painted by the smooth-talking recruitment agents. Covered in soot and grime, with hollow eyes and hunched shoulders, the workers presented a pitiful sight—broken men who bore on their backs the crushing weight of industrial progress.

The newcomers realized with growing horror that they were looking at their own immediate fate. Like all unskilled and illiterate newcomers, they would have to start at the very bottom of the socio-economic ladder.

Reluctantly, the brotherhood of Slavs parted ways.

Michal and Juraj turned and marched on toward Duquesne. However dispirited they were, they could not afford to wallow in their disappointment. If they had to gather buckets of coal, instead of nuggets of gold, then so be it.

To their great relief, with thousands of their compatriots from Šariš, Zemplín, and Spiš preceding them to Pittsburgh, the ground had already been prepared for them. Luck smiled at the friends when they found lodging in a crowded boarding house run by a sharp-tongued Rusyn matron[13] who, charmed by Michal's manners, agreed to take in Juraj as well. It was important to win a landlady's favor for she would pack their lunch pails, wash and mend their clothes, and shepherd them through their first bewildering months in America.

---

[13] The women who ran the boarding houses made a real contribution to easing the transition to life in America.

The next morning, despite their bodies crying out for rest, they forced themselves back onto their blistered, cloth-bound feet.

Debts wouldn't pay themselves, and their families back home couldn't eat promises.

Still wearing their travel-stained *kroje*, the two men ventured out to find employment. They quickly learned why locals referred to the town's steepest section as Coal Hill. Mines, large and small, dotted the elevated landscape.

The Duquesne Mine, operated by the Corey Coal Company, hired them on the spot—adding two more Slavic names to a daily labor roster of 120 men. However, the promise of immediate work came with a catch.

Juraj and Michal could report to work as soon as they purchased the necessary mining equipment. The bad news was that they would have to pay for this equipment out of their own pockets.

The company would not provide the men with the necessary tools—a shovel, a helmet, even a simple bucket. The so-called "good news" was that all the mandatory equipment could be conveniently purchased at the nearby company store—and the cost would then be neatly deducted from the migrant's wages.

Juraj's heart sank as he studied the inflated prices. Nearly a week's wages gone before he even set foot in the mine! And that was only for the bare minimum of equipment. It was yet another blow to his fading dream of El Dorado.

The very next morning, the two men stood side by side at the mine's entrance, peering into its hungry darkness.

"Is this what we left behind the fields and forests of our homeland for? Is this the price of the American dream?"

The questions echoed silently between them, heavier than the tools they carried, and with no clear answer to be heard.

The Dark Depths
PITTSBURGH, 1895

Dear Reader, in the 1890s, descending into a coal mine meant risking your life. Mining was one of the most dangerous jobs in the world because, in the cruel mathematics of American industry, miners were as disposable as the tools they wielded.

The country's growth depended on the relentless supply of "black gold" and the cheap labor needed to dig it out of the earth. At the peak of the Great Industrial Revolution, no one cared if a miner lived or died.

The endless stream of immigrants arriving on America's shores ensured a perpetual supply of desperate men willing to take the places of the dead and the crippled. All for a chance at providing a better life and future for their families in Europe.

Even those who survived with all their limbs attached paid a steep toll later on. Years of inhaling coal dust led many men to develop what was known as black lung, a merciless disease that slowly suffocated its victims, turning their final years into a desperate struggle for breath.

To Anna, Juraj was the center of her world, but to his employers, he was merely a number in their ledger. While she prayed daily for his safe return, they calculated his worth in tons of coal he extracted.

The Duquesne mine, perched on Coal Hill, had earned a reputation as one of the safer operations—a distinction that spoke more to the horrors of the other mines than to any virtue of its own. That year, the Duquesne mine was spared any fatal accidents.

Although far from the promised land of his dreams, Coal Hill offered Juraj the opportunity to earn as much in one day as he could have earned in weeks, even months, in Upper Hungary.

And so, day by day, he descended into the darkness, measuring his progress toward freedom in one-dollar-and-fifty-cent increments. It was a daily wage that no self-respecting American would have accepted. Yet for the likes of Juraj, the grueling twelve-hour shifts and six-day workweeks were a sacrifice he had to make.

Juraj was used to working hard, so it wasn't the labor that tormented him. What haunted Juraj was where he worked.

The narrow, dark, damp tunnels felt like a coffin to this farmer who was accustomed to working in fields, in forests, and under wide-open skies. In the mines, Juraj started work early and ended late, so sometimes weeks would pass before he even caught a glimpse of daylight.

Is it any wonder that after a long day of backbreaking labor, the miners sought comfort in the murky saloons that lined their path home?

The streets were dotted with bars and taverns, each offering a brief escape. A glass, or a few, of cheap American whiskey made the world feel brighter for the weary immigrant, if only for a little while.

Unlike countless Slovaks who turned to alcohol to escape the grim reality, Juraj maintained his resolve, swearing on the memory of his father to stay away from the saloons altogether. After each shift, while his colleagues stumbled into the taverns, Juraj walked straight back to the boarding house, where he shared a narrow bunkbed with Michal.

Every penny saved brought Juraj one step closer to his golden target: $1,000—the price of returning to Slovakia not as a survivor, but as a wealthy man.

A Miner's Prayer
PITTSBURGH, 1895

While dreams of returning home sustained Juraj during the endless days and lonely nights, Pittsburgh nevertheless slowly became a home.

The city's Slovak quarter was growing, and each new arrival brought with them a little piece of the Old Country. Here, matrons dressed in colorful headscarves and white aprons organized neighborhood social events. Familiar sounds echoed off the brick walls of the two-story houses. The scents of home—steaming cabbage rolls, cooked sausages, and freshly baked bread—wafted from basement kitchens.

The newly arrived Slovaks had carved out spaces of their own not just in Pennsylvania's steel city, but across the northeast. Like scattered seeds taking root, Slovak shops, clubs, taverns, and fraternal societies reflected the size of the growing community.

The timing couldn't have been more fortuitous for Juraj. In October 1895, mere weeks before his arrival, the first Slovak church in Pittsburgh opened its doors and had soon established itself at the heart of the local immigrant world.

Standing proudly on the corner of 15th Street and Pennsylvania Avenue, the newly erected church was dedicated to St. Elizabeth of Hungary, a patron saint of the poor who was beloved by Slavs all over Europe.

It was a testament to the unwavering faith and determination of Slovak immigrants who achieved what had seemed impossible—building their own house of worship from the dismal wages, earned one penny at a time in the mines and mills of Pittsburgh.

No immigrant church was complete without a priest who could serve mass in one's native language. The Slovak community was successful yet again, recruiting a kind and wise man from Upper Hungary to serve their spiritual needs.

Now, every Sunday, the Slovaks could whisper their prayers and make their confessions in their mother tongue—a great comfort for the souls aching for home and struggling with the reality of life in America.

The appearance of this sanctuary assured Juraj that God was with him every step of the way, even in this foreign land. The Sunday pilgrimage to mass across Pittsburgh became a beacon of hope in his otherwise monotonous and dark week. But it did require a small sacrifice.

Try as he might to avoid spending money on anything that was not essential, the steep slope of Coal Hill proved impossible for Juraj's legs, already weary from six-days of shifts each week. With its rhythmic creaking and gentle sway, the electric trolley car that took him up the Duquesne incline became his reluctant chariot to heaven. Juraj felt that attending the Catholic mass was worth every hard-earned penny he spent to get there.

The familiar hymns in Slovak comforted Juraj deeply, and for a brief moment, he could close his eyes and imagine Anna beside him, their shoulders touching as they knelt side by side in prayer.

Dear Reader, the Slovak church in Pittsburgh became more than a refuge to Juraj—it opened the door to possibilities he had never imagined.

Beneath its vaulted ceilings, a different kind of gift was offered after Sunday service: the gift of literacy. When the other miners sought solace in whiskey, Juraj spent his evenings and humble earnings learning to read and write in Slovak.

His coal-stained fingers practiced tracing the unfamiliar letters, one determined pen stroke at a time. The photograph of Anna, tucked safely in his Bible, seemed to smile with pride at his efforts.

If he couldn't be with his family, he would at least make every moment of separation count by bettering himself.

Still, the loneliness pressed against his tired mind in the quiet hours after his studies. That is when he would carefully remove the photograph from its holy shelter and gently trace the contours of her beautiful face with his rough fingers, imagining breathing in her rosy scent. How he longed to kiss her and hear the laughter of his children! They must have grown so much in his absence.

For Slovaks, who counted wealth not in dollars but in family bonds, being separated from loved ones was like being cut off from oxygen—not just painful but wholly unnatural.

To console himself, Juraj would stroke the handkerchief-wrapped Slovak soil, close his eyes and summon the feeling of home through all his senses. From the pungent smell of manure in the stable to the sweet aroma of Anna's cooking, from the smoky scent of the firewood in the evenings to the earthy fragrance of the fields in spring.

Juraj recalled their little *drevenica* with astonishing clarity—the way the front door creaked announcing every coming and going and the familiar rattle of the tiny windows on windy nights.

But his favorite daydream was always of his return to Slovakia.

In this cherished fantasy, he fleshed out the triumphant moment in great detail—how he would stroll confidently into Krivany, dressed in a dashing American suit, a fine hat atop his head. An elegant travel trunk would carry wonders that he would be able to give to his loved ones.

He imagined how the children would run up ahead, spreading the news, and the neighbors would emerge from their homes with broad smiles and calls of *"Vitaj doma, Juraj!"*

Anna would be waiting for him at the doorstep of their cottage, throwing herself into his arms and covering his face with kisses. How proud she would be when he spread the crisp American banknotes across the table: one thousand US dollars! A fortune for their family!

Juraj clung to these visions with all his heart and soul.

Each swift swing of his pickaxe, each letter diligently mastered, and each hard-earned penny saved brought him one step closer to turning that blessed dream into reality.

A loud snore of a fellow boarder suddenly brought him back to reality. For now, he would have to endure the separation, the backbreaking work, and the endless longing for his wife, family, and home.

Anna's Ordeal
KRIVANY, 1895

In Upper Hungary, Anna faced challenges of her own.

With Juraj gone, the weight of the responsibility for the household, field, and children settled on her shoulders. Every dawn was a test of her strength and resolve—carrying heavy water buckets from the well, chopping firewood for the stove, shoveling manure from the barn. Her hands, once soft and dainty enough for delicate embroidery, grew calloused and raw.

Yet every morning, she forced herself out of bed to face another day without Juraj, knowing full well that the farm and children wouldn't wait for her while she pitied herself.

Anna had been just sixteen when she had married Juraj. He was a handsome and kind man, and she was deeply honored when he asked her parents for permission to propose to her.

During the long winter evenings, as Anna's needle danced across the fabric, stitching her wedding *kroj* by candlelight, she could not have imagined a greater happiness than marrying the man of her dreams and sharing a life by his side.

When the day finally came and she walked down the church aisle wearing the *kroj* she had sewn her hopes and dreams into, Juraj's gaze met hers with such love, it nearly stopped her heart.

The vows the couple exchanged at the altar were sacred. They promised to stand by each other's side in sickness and in health, in wealth and in poverty.

Their love was genuine, steadfast, and unconditional, but now an ocean divided what no human force was meant to separate.

When doubt or pity crept in, Anna would remind herself that every burden she shouldered alone was another coin saved. Every lonely night was one step closer toward her reunion with her beloved.

She was not alone in her ordeal. Krivany, like so many other villages scattered across the hills and valleys of eastern Slovakia, had become a place of waiting women.

In the prolonged absence of husbands, even the strongest marriages began to crack.

Whispers slipped between cottage walls of wives who, crushed by loneliness, sought comfort in the arms of others, of children born out of wedlock, and of the poor husband's despair upon returning to his family.

Even in tiny Krivany, where no secret could be contained for long, women succumbed to temptations. The Slovak countryside shunned such behavior. There was no place for these women and the children they bore, except at the very edge of society. They became outcasts.

Anna's heart ached for these women who were living with the fruits of their desperate choices. She wept too for their distant husbands, laboring in foreign lands, unaware of the broken vows and consequences.

Though suitors circled around her like hungry wolves, drawn by her beauty and her dignified strength, Anna's devotion to Juraj never wavered.

"How could I love a man this much?" Anna whispered to herself in the dead of the night.

In moments when her solitude threatened to swallow her whole, Anna found refuge in her grandmother's prayers. At dawn and dusk, she was on her knees, reciting prayers for Juraj's safety and for the wind that would carry him back, across the vast ocean.

She couldn't have known that each word became a thread of invisible armor, wrapping itself around Juraj. Her pure love created a spiritual shield against the menacing blackness of the deep American shafts.

So powerful is human love.

Letters from Home

KRIVANY AND PITTSBURGH, 1895

The seasons turned. Juraj's first year in America was coming to an end, and his savings were growing.

Each evening, after washing the coal dust from his body, he'd perform his sacred ritual of counting his American money. Every penny felt like a promise kept, bringing him closer to that mythical thousand dollars, which would transform him from a coal-covered immigrant in America into a respected landowner back home.

But America's promises proved slower to fulfill than he'd hoped and only letters from home brightened the lonely monotony of life at Coal Hill.

The Slovak literacy classes Juraj was taking turned out to be one of the smartest investments he made. Though heartsick for home, he could at least bridge the vast Atlantic with his words.

He ended each letter with "I love and miss you dearly," and Anna answered with unfailing devotion: "We are waiting for you, my love, come home quickly."

Each of Anna's letters traveled across the ocean for weeks, sometimes even months. But when it finally arrived, it carried more than just news from home. Tucked inside were illustrations and pressed wildflowers from the Slovak meadows.

Each white envelope, adorned with stamps from the Kingdom of Hungary, was for Juraj a sacred treasure—a tangible piece of home—that he treated with the reverence of a holy relic.

Anna, on the other hand, could neither read nor write.

It was the nine-year-old Jakub who, to everyone's great surprise, became Juraj's messenger to his wife. Despite Jakub's patchy schooling, the boy had mastered enough letters to decipher his father's words and to pen down his mother's instructions, proving to both parents the inestimable value of education.

In the flickering light of the evening stove, Jakub stood like a priest before his congregation. His chest puffed with pride as he sounded out the words, bringing Juraj's writings to life while his mother and sister leaned forward, hungry to learn more about Papa's adventures in America.

On some quiet evenings, neighbors would come in as well, clutching their own envelopes, creased and smudged from many handlings. Children sat cross-legged by the stove, the elders on the bench, all eager to catch every word.

One by one, the letters were unfolded and read aloud.

Voices carried the words across the room—sometimes halting and trembling, sometimes proud and bright—giving life to these precious dispatches from a far-off land.

Stories from distant coal towns and steel mills echoed through the room, intertwining with sighs, laughter, and the occasional quiet tear.

"My brother is digging alongside your son in Duquesne."

"My cousin is sending for his wife—they'll be living in Chicago by spring."

"My son has found work… and maybe even love."

In a world divided by distance, these scraps of paper stitched their world back together with stories. In the telling and retelling of these stories, their hope grew stronger, passed from heart to heart the way a warm loaf of bread might be passed hand to hand on a cold winter night.

Yet, Dear Reader, letters, precious as they were, the stories couldn't fill the void of empty arms.

After a year of solitude, Juraj finally pushed open the door of his first American saloon.

Perhaps we can forgive this moment of weakness. After all, Juraj was not only a determined father and a loving husband. He was also human.

Inside the dim saloon, the air buzzed with the familiar sounds of home. Slovak miners raised their glasses of cheap whiskey, their laughter blending with fragments of old folk songs. Nostalgia hung thick in the smoky air—sweet, heavy, and just the alcohol, just enough to dull.

When liquor warmed Juraj and loosened the knot in his chest, twelve months of unshed tears finally broke free. To mask the emotion swelling inside him, he reached for his harmonica and began to play, pouring his heartache into every trembling note.

He could not have known that darkness was already gathering on the horizon—a storm that would soon test him like never before, pushing him to the very edge of his strength.

The Last Shift
COAL HILL, JANUARY 1896

One grey January morning, tragedy shattered the miners' drab and dreary routine. It happened during Juraj's shift. The coal cart, usually steady on its iron rails, jolted violently. It had caught on something—a stray timber, a loose stone, no one could say for sure. The shriek of metal grinding against metal tore through the darkness.

"What's happening?" Juraj asked. His heart was pounding wildly and mind was racing to make sense of it as he turned toward the sound. His lamp's dim glow caught Michal's face—eyes wide, frozen in panic.

Then came the crack. A sickening snap of splintering wood echoed through the shaft as one of the support beams gave way. The overloaded cart rocked, then tipped.

Michal, his dear Rusyn friend and brother in exile, didn't even have time to cry out.

The cart's thunderous crash echoed through the underground chambers, a sound so brutal that it seemed to cut through the earth itself. It was followed by a deafening silence.

Alone in that terrible moment, Juraj reached for Michal's broken body, so full of zest for life just moments ago. Now, it lay limp and lifeless in his arms.

Time disappeared, minutes could have been hours, and hours became eternities. The world above ceased to exist. All that remained was the dark void and the shock at what had just happened.

The only sound punctuating the oppressive nothingness was Juraj's ragged breaths as he carried Michal's body out of the doomed shaft. Near the surface, other miners emerged from the darkness to join the grim procession.

Together, they carried their fallen brother into the drizzly afternoon.

Juraj's face was ghostly pale, and his eyes were haunted by the horrors still unraveling in his mind. He whispered, "*Otčenáš*"[14] beneath his breath.

Each fragile word of the Lord's Prayer was both a plea and a lament—a trembling attempt to bridge the chasm between hope and despair, between the living and the dead.

Back home, death had its ceremony. The whole village would gather and sing funeral hymns that carried the soul to heaven. The great church bell would toll across the valley, deep and mournful, offering one final farewell on behalf of the departed to all who had known them.

"But here?" Juraj thought bitterly. "Here, men die like animals."

The mine management dismissed the death as an unfortunate incident. After all, a single fatality fell well within the acceptable parameters of the Duquesne operation

---

14 The Lord's Prayer

for the year. The company didn't like losing men, but one dead immigrant barely registered—a ripple in the relentless tide of industrial progress.

The mining company offered no prayer and no acknowledgement—only a wagon ride. Michal's lifeless body was dropped at his lodging, left for the neighbors to handle. They would have to wash and dress the dead, to scrape together what they could for a funeral, and to shoulder the sorrowful duty of writing home to the family in the Old Country.

Juraj was expected to return to work as if nothing had happened. As if Michal hadn't been the one who kept his spirits buoyed through those long, punishing twelve-hour shifts in the darkness. With a quiet smile, a kind word, or an unexpected joke, Michal made their twelve-hour shifts pass just a little bit quicker.

Michal was gone. Forever.

Juraj's world was turned upside down, and no prayer could quiet the guilt that crept into the young man's heart.

Hell with the Lid Off
PITTSBURGH, 1896

In the days that followed, Juraj saw the mine as a haunting mausoleum where water dripped like tears from the low, dark tunnels. Juraj saw Michal's face in every shadow and heard his laughter echoing in every hollow chamber.

The damp darkness that had taken his friend now seemed to reach for Juraj's spirit—hungry to devour another immigrant soul.

One morning, long before the first light of day, Juraj had to face the somber reality. He couldn't return to the ill-fated mine. Duquesne had become unbearable, and Coal Hill, with its grim promises and tragic memories, offered him nothing but a future stained with grief.

Thankfully, finding new work was easy in those days, and Juraj did not have to look for long.

The imposing silhouette of the Edgar Thomson Steel Works in Braddock, his new place of work, now loomed before him. Hoping for a fresh start, Juraj moved into another boarding house perched on the hill above the steelworks.

But neither the crowded house, nor the Monongahela River that rushed past, nor the mill's deafening cacophony could drown out the memory of the piercing scream, the sickening thud of a body hitting the ground, and the mortal silence that had followed Michal's death.

In one devastating moment, his friend's life and dreams crumbled into dust. His vision of returning to Slovakia and purchasing a carpenter's workshop, which Michal had shared so often over their humble suppers, was extinguished forever.

He would never again embrace his wife and children.

Confronted by Michal's cruel fate, the only thing Juraj could do was to trudge forward. His refuge from grief became his work—a monotonous cycle of tasks amid the hiss of steam and the suffocating heat of furnaces. All of this required just enough of Juraj's attention to keep his mind from wandering. It was a fragile shield against despair—but it was a shield nevertheless.

The steel mill might have been less treacherous than the mine, but it offered its own version of hell. Blazing furnaces roared like hungry dragons, their breath so hot it could sear a man's lungs. Endless shifts in the infernal heat felt like being inside a caldron beside the devil himself.

Yet, Juraj barely felt the discomfort. Since his friend's death, Juraj had become numb to everything except the ever-present guilt.

He embraced the despised night shifts as punishment and shouldered whatever additional burdens his colleagues heaped upon him without protest. The flames could lick his skin, and the molten steel could burn his arms—he was indifferent to it all.

Juraj had trapped himself in a purgatory of his own making. "Why Michal? Why not me?" The pointless question tortured his mind day and night.

Wrestling with God
PITTSBURGH, 1896

Gone were the days when Juraj resisted the lure of liquor. Though he kept the promise he had made to his family to work hard and earn money, the alcohol took a terrible toll.

The taverns outside the mill beckoned with voices more compelling than prayer. The dim saloons became his sanctuary, where the clink of glasses and whiskey's familiar burn offered fleeting moments of escape, even as his savings dwindled.

One glass was never enough to push the pain back into the darkest recesses of his mind. Soon, the bitter taste of cheap alcohol became as much a part of his daily routine as the hissing fire and ceaseless clang of the mill's machinery.

Days bled into nights, as the world turned black for Juraj. Evenings blurred into obscurity, ending only when the bartender's annoyed voice broke through his drunken haze, refusing to serve him another round.

Staggering into the cold streets, Juraj found his way back to the boarding house on the better nights, collapsing onto the stiff mattress and blacking out. On other, less forgiving nights he'd wake in a dark alley or on an abandoned park bench, his clothes soiled, his pockets emptied, his head throbbing with regret.

Yet, each morning, he'd rise mechanically, a shell of a man caught in an endless cycle of work, drink, and oblivion—each moment a futile attempt to escape the agony of his guilt. No amount of labor or liquor could silence the impossible question, *Why not me?*

The Slovak church, once an anchor that kept him from drifting with the currents, became unbearably painful. Every familiar ritual and prayer felt like an accusation: *Why not me?* The social gatherings that had once offered comfort now stood only as a reminder that he had failed to save his friend.

Writing home was unimaginable.

Whenever he closed his eyes, he saw Michal's cobalt blue eyes that sparkled with life and unbridled enthusiasm. How could he write to his own wife when he couldn't bring himself to write to Michal's widow of her husband's death?

Dear Reader, imagine the painful contrast between Juraj's past and present.

He'd left behind the green hills and lush forests of eastern Slovakia, a world where community, faith, and family were the cornerstones and safeguards of existence.

Now, he found himself living in a netherworld where a human life was valued less than the coal the immigrants mined or the steel they forged.

This is how Pittsburgh earned its infamous moniker, "hell with the lid off." Here, men were nothing but cogs in the great industrial machine, sacrificed daily on the altar of progress. Juraj's heart became embittered. America was no longer a wonderland where dreams come true; it was a place of false promises.

In the gloom that surrounded him, only one light remained—the unconditional love of his family.

Memories of his wife and children in Krivany were Juraj's last tether to sanity. Their faces alone could chase away the demons that haunted his days and consumed his nights.

But time was slipping away.

A year and a half passed since he had kissed his loved ones goodbye.

The Power of Love

KRIVANY, SPRING 1896

In the depths of the Carpathian forest, Anna felt that something was amiss. Her twenty-sixth birthday came and went without a single word from her husband. It had been months since she heard from him.

Every Tuesday morning, she paced the picket fence that marked their tiny garden, searching for the first sign of the postman. And every Tuesday, she prayed that he would have an envelope with Juraj's writing on it. But week after week, the postman walked past, offering only a sympathetic shrug:

"Maybe next week, Anna. Maybe next week."

Anna didn't know if Juraj had found another woman, if he'd become sick or injured—or if he was dead. Refusing to let the distress devour her, Anna devoted herself ever more fervently to her faith.

Whenever she could get away from the endless procession of duties, chores, and childcare, she would run to the white-washed church at the village square.

As her fears grew more intense, so did her pleas. "*Prosím, Bože,*[15] keep my Juraj safe," she prayed as she lit a candle at the altar of the Virgin Mary, hoping that its light would guide her husband safely home.

But three months of silence turned into six, and still there was no news from Juraj.

Worse, the tales of golden opportunities in America gave way to stories of the true fate of Slovaks in the New World. After Sunday church, Anna overheard a group of neighbors whispering about a woman from another village who had lost her only son to an American coal mine.

The news struck Anna like a thunderbolt.

Was that why letters stopped coming? What if Juraj, too, was gone? Panic swelled in her chest at the thought of her children growing up fatherless, a future too devastating to entertain even for a moment.

As Anna clenched her trembling hands, courage surged through her, turning fear into fierce determination. Her beloved Ďurko—a pet name she loved to call him—was alive! She knew it; she felt it in every fiber of her being.

Dear Reader, you are about to witness the power of a woman's love—a love that would soon set our heroine on an unexpected path. This path came into being thanks to the "American fever" that was then sweeping through Upper Hungary.

The conservative Slovak countryside was changing fast. What had begun as a trickle of pioneers leaving for abroad

---

[15] Please, God.

rapidly turned into a mighty exodus. By the end of the 19th century, eastern Slovak villages were nearly empty of men.

Unexpectedly, the era gave Slovak women a taste of freedom and sovereignty. With the men gone, the women had to step forward, making decisions, managing resources, and taking charge of the future.

When the women shouldered the responsibilities of men, they began to uncover a strength and resilience they had never before known that they possessed. No longer confined to the role of caretakers and homemakers, they were now in charge of overseeing households and farms, becoming the main supports for their families and their communities.

Before long, these very same women began to wonder about the world beyond their village borders. Why couldn't they, too, chase the same dreams of prosperity as the men around them had done? If their husbands, fathers, and brothers could leave, so could they.

Seven years before, in 1879, the first group of brave women set sail on a steamship bound for America. They had settled in New Jersey, finding work in its booming textile factories, and word of their success spread across Slovak villages, inspiring more women to follow in their footsteps.

Some women dreamed of modern houses, and some had more expanded notions of what they could accomplish by crossing the ocean. Some wanted to strike it rich in America and return home as free women. Some wanted to strike it rich in America and return home as free women, able to choose their husbands—a radical notion in the

Slovak countryside, where marriages were arranged for pragmatic reasons and often set in place generations beforehand. With American dollars in hand, local village girls aspired to break free from the way things had always been done and to make their own decisions about their lives.

These female trailblazers became Anna's beacon of hope, and when letter after letter they wrote went unanswered by Juraj, she resolved to take matters into her own hands.

She would go to America and find him.

To accomplish this, Anna would need every ounce of determination she could muster. She needed not one but three steamship tickets. Where would she find the money for such an expense? And even if she did, how would she prepare for such a daunting journey without her husband's advice or strength?

Paralyzed by uncertainty, resolved to put her plan into action, but completely unsure about how she could manage, Anna received a surprising message from a cousin that she saw as divine providence.

She learned that a group of women and children was leaving for America in just two months and that she could join them. The difficult part of this was that this didn't leave her she much time to buy the steamship tickets and to figure out what to do with her family's house and field.

There wasn't a moment to waste. Anna began by selling the remaining livestock, praying that she would get a fair price at the market. Next, she sold whatever household items she could spare. She even took on an extra job as a cook for the village mayor. Still, the coins she earned felt like drops in an ocean, far from enough for a single transatlantic ticket, let alone three.

It didn't seem possible that she could accomplish this, yet she had to try. And giving into despair was a luxury that Anna could not afford.

Desperate Times Call for Desperate Measures

KRIVANY, JUNE 1896

One evening, as silence settled over the house, Anna climbed into the attic, taking with her a single candle against the darkness. Her fingers trembled with both hope and dread as she rummaged through an old wooden chest.

Beneath the layers of faded linens, she found what she was looking for: her mother's ruby pendant. It was a delicate, timeworn piece of gold—a thick gold frame cradled a single deep dark, red ruby that gleamed with almost defiant intensity. Etched into the surface of the ruby, lovingly and with impossible precision, was an intricate carving of the Virgin Mary. Encircling the sacred image, in tiny, flowing script, was an inscription in Latin—*In tenebris lucet* (she shines in the darkness).

The gem and its message—one of fire, one of faith—had been in her family for generations, and no one knew how humble peasants came to possess such a treasure. Perhaps a forbidden love story, a great many years ago? Or an expression of gratitude for a life saved or a secret kept by a Hungarian noble? Whatever the reason, the thought of parting with this family heirloom felt like a knife to the heart.

But she was running out of time and options.

Tears welled as she clutched the pendant and whispered into the stillness, "Forgive me. I will carry your memory, even without this."

The next day, Anna made her way to the town's inn. The innkeeper was the only man she knew who was wealthy enough to buy the necklace from her.

The innkeeper immediately recognized the pendant's exceptional value—far beyond the price of the three steerage tickets Anna needed. He could already imagine showing it to his acquaintance in Budapest, a collector of rare treasures who would pay quite handsomely for such a find—perhaps double what Anna was asking.

For a moment, her haunted expression gave him pause. But only for a moment. His calculating mind quickly overrode any flicker of conscience. This was a golden opportunity, and greed, not mercy, would guide his hand.

"I'll buy it," he said smoothly, "but the pendant alone won't be enough to cover your steamship tickets." The lie slid effortlessly off his tongue. "I'll lend you the remaining money—on one condition."

Anna's heart ached, and her body stiffened. "What condition?" she asked, her voice trembling beneath the weight of dread.

"I shall require your house as surety for the debt," the innkeeper replied before quickly scribbling a contract.

Her stomach sank. "The house?" The ominous words hung in the stuffy tavern air.

The terms were clear and harsh. If she failed to repay the loan within one year, the Sobota home would be his. Torn between two impossible choices, Anna's hands hovered over the contract. Her heart raced. Although she could not read, she could identify her name in print.

The homestead built by her father represented more than just wood and stone. It was memories of her parents, Juraj's love, her children's laughter, quiet moments of peace. Yet, the prospect of facing another month without her Juraj was unbearable.

Anna swallowed her fear, gripped the quill, and signed the document with a cross—a bold and unthinkable act for a young woman of her time.

With that single action, she was risking everything: her family's land, her children's future, and the only home they had ever known, for the man she loved.

For Anna, the desire to reunite her family was greater than her fear of losing the monumental gamble she had taken.

Once she had the money in her hand, events unfolded fast. As a woman, Anna was spared the military conscription that had complicated her husband's departure, and so her path to America was clear of bureaucratic hurdles.

Within a week, the group of Slovak women and children stood in Bremen, Germany. Storm clouds were gathering on the horizon.

The port roared with life: a cacophony of foreign tongues, towering steamships, and—for Anna—emotions too big for her to name. A fierce wind tugged at Anna's headscarf as she stared out at the vast, forbidding ocean that stretched endlessly before her. In that moment, she felt both awestruck and profoundly lost.

Jakub and Marienka clung to their mother's voluminous skirts, their wide eyes mirroring her own, a mixture of terror and wonder as they beheld the deep blue unknown that looked as if it were waiting to swallow them whole.

Amidst the chaos of departure, the band of Slovak women became Anna's quiet source of strength, offering comfort that went beyond words. In one another, these women found something precious: a lifeline to the world they were leaving behind and a wellspring of courage for the uncertain journey ahead.

Most, like Anna, were on their way to reunite with husbands who had gone before them. Others were single maidens, bravely setting out for America in search of work—as factory girls, seamstresses, or maids in unfamiliar households.

For the next fourteen days aboard the ship, they would become more than fellow travelers. They would become family.

PART 3
REUNITED

Out on the Ocean
THE ATLANTIC, JULY 1896

The Atlantic crossing etched itself into each passenger's memories in different ways. For Anna, the days stretched endlessly, each filled with stories that made the blood freeze in her veins.

Between the gentle tugs of hair-braiding and quiet murmurs, the women shared stories that haunted their nights—tales of mines that devoured men, leaving behind a trail of tears and forsaken widows.

They spoke of mysterious sicknesses that stole breath and of men who found refuge from their fears in bottles of whiskey. Every week, they said, another soul wouldn't return home to his family, swallowed by a hungry mine or crushed by unforgiving machinery.

Anna wondered, "Why does God demand such a sacrifice for a better life?"

In the silence of the night, she pressed Juraj's letters to her chest, searching her memory for hints of danger among his hopeful words. But he had carefully hidden from her the sad destinies of Slovak men in America.

On the other hand, for Jakub and Marienka, the ship was a floating wonderland. The two children were living the adventure of a lifetime!

They reveled in the exhilarating experiences aboard the gigantic streamliner, where everything was new, exciting, and fun. When they raced each other across the deck, seagulls soaring overhead, the salty breeze tussling their hair, their enthusiasm was as boundless as the horizon before them.

Day after day, they studied the deep wide blue for the "big fish." How thrilled they were when they finally spotted their first blue whale! Seeing it was even more magnificent than hearing about it had been in their father's letters.

The children squealed with joy as the massive back arched elegantly above the waterline and then disappeared into the deep again.

But the marvels of the voyage didn't end there. The spectacle of the refined first-class passengers strolling about the upper deck above them was also entertaining for the youngsters. Gracious ladies glided across the deck in exquisite dresses, their precious jewels catching the light and scattering tiny rainbows across their necks and hands. Gentlemen, in immaculate three-piece suits, tipped their top hats at the bejeweled ladies with practiced ease.

The children had never seen such wealth before. Seeing such luxuriousness firsthand was like peering into a fairytale. Together, they whispered and giggled as they imagined walking among those grand people for a day.

One Hungarian lady, noticing their wide-eyed wonder, presented them with strange yellow fruit, and Marienka nearly swooned with excitement.

The siblings dutifully brought the treasure to their mother, causing their entire section in steerage to gather to inspect the exotic bananas, and debate how to eat them.

"With the peel or without it?" pondered the troop of Slovak women.

After some deliberation, Anna removed the peel and cautiously took a first bite. Her soft gasp of delight hinted at the exotic wonders that awaited in the New World.

For Anna, the commotion in the bowels of the ship was a welcome distraction to an otherwise dull routine. Not used to being idle, she and the other Slovak women found themselves secretly looking forward to the torturously long mealtime rituals.

At breakfast, lunch, and dinner, she shepherded the children into the austere dining hall to queue up for a good part of an hour. The reward was a mediocre meal devoid of the slightest trace of love. To make matters worse, there were never enough seats to go around.

But Mama Sobota made a game of it.

Jakub would circle the dining hall like a hawk, scanning the crowded room for an opening at one of the long, communal tables. Once he spotted a place, Marienka would dart in to secure their hard-won territory, her small frame holding firm among the sea of travelers.

Soon after, their mother would appear, balancing three dented metal bowls—each filled with a ladle of lukewarm porridge or some unrecognizable stew. It wasn't much, but the children smiled nevertheless, as if it were a feast.

The bland meals were followed by a daily ordeal of washing up the spoons and bowls at the single water tap. An equally long queue followed, but after the unsatisfying meal, it was an even greater trial of their patience than lining up for food.

As inconvenient as the mealtime perils were, they offered a strange comfort to Anna. At least it was something to do besides endlessly worrying about Juraj.

Watching her fellow passengers push the colorless blobs of food around the plates, Anna thanked herself for her foresight in packing extra provisions—smoked cheese, bacon, and a few loaves of tangy sourdough. Whenever the steerage meal was not enough, she carefully rationed the supplies to make the wholesome food last, often sacrificing her portion so her children could eat their fill.

Perhaps it was God's protective hand that kept the seas calm throughout their journey. Without any storms marring their passage, the voyage unfurled as an uneventful procession of days that blurred together in an endless cycle of meals, prayers, and whispered stories, before the long and rocky nights.

But with each sunrise, anticipation grew as the ship edged closer to America.

After thirteen days at sea, Jakub spotted a shoreline.

Bittersweet Arrival
NEW YORK, JULY 1896

"Land!" the boy cried as he raced below deck, nearly tumbling down the stairs and into the dim steerage quarters. "We've arrived!"

When Lady Liberty emerged from the morning haze, Jakub and Marienka pressed against the ship's railing, forgetting to close their mouths, so hypnotized were they by the sight. The statue's torch pierced the fog like a beacon, her silent welcome already legendary among the immigrants.

It was hard to believe that they, humble folk from a tiny Slovak village, now stood in her presence.

The confident smile of Lady Liberty was a promise even to Anna—exhausted though she was by weeks of travel and worry—that the future had good things in store for them. Yet she could not shake off the feeling of anxiety as their ship glided into the bustling city harbor.

In steerage, passengers scrambled to gather their belongings, desperate to feel solid ground beneath their feet once again. With their provisions gone, Anna did not have much to pack, and before she knew it, they were boarding a ferry to Ellis Island.

With bated breath, she watched the sprawling red-brick complex. During the long voyage, Anna heard many horrific stories about the immigration procedures. Luckily, she wouldn't have to face the officers alone.

A seasoned Ukrainian matron who had made this journey before took the Slovak women and children under her wing, guiding them through the intimidating maze of medical inspections and questioning.

Safely on the other side, the farewells came too soon.

Happiness that the journey had ended was mingled with the sadness of saying goodbye. It was a bittersweet moment for the band of women who had shared cramped quarters and precious food. They had helped rock each other's crying children to sleep and whispered prayers in difficult moments, while empowering each other to keep going.

Unlike the women who flew into the open arms of their husbands, relatives, or friends, Anna stood alone on the dock. She watched the joyful reunions around her with an ache in her chest. She knew that no familiar face would emerge from the crowd to greet them. She drew Jakubko and Marienka close, vowing to find their father, no matter what it took.

She had crossed the ocean on hope alone, and now she would have to navigate this mysterious land on her own.

A Mother's Courage
NEW YORK, JULY 1896

Looking around the docks bustling with passengers, merchants, agents, officers, and crooks, Anna weighed her options. All she had of Juraj's whereabouts was the address in Pennsylvania.

Spotting a group heading toward Manhattan's train station, she joined their steady flow. The children, with their small feet and short legs, hurried behind her to match the pace of the adults. They knew better than to complain.

The grandest train station Anna had ever seen in Bremen, was now paled by comparison to the imposing Grand Central Depot. The American flag flapped dramatically over the roof of the massive building, which hummed with energy. Inside, the hubbub of voices revealed a surprise. The vast hall was filled with people speaking languages that sounded familiar to Anna!

Drawn to the sound of recognizable words, Anna found other Slavic migrants who, like herself, were traveling to Pennsylvania.

"Pit-z-burg," Jakub sounded out the word inscribed on the platform while his mother pondered a more pressing challenge.

The last of their coins had been spent on food in the docks—two baloney sandwiches for the children. In truth, she could only afford to buy one, but the vendor took pity on the thin woman with two hungry children beside her. With a soft smile and nod, he gave her two sandwiches for the price of one. Grateful, Anna watched Jakubko and Marienka devour their first American meal.

But now her purse was empty.

The train to Pittsburgh was already at the platform, its whistle piercing the afternoon air. When the conductor shouted, "All aboard!" the impatient crowd pushed forward in waves, leaving Anna no time to dwell on her money dilemma.

The frightened woman gripped her children's hands and moved with the human tide, watching and mimicking the other passengers as they received destination boards around their necks.

The third-class cars were heaving with passengers, each scuttling to claim one of the last free seats. There were none left for Anna and her little ones, so she tucked her family into a nook by the door in the narrow passageway.

It would have to do. Holding her children close to her, Anna closed her eyes and prayed that the journey would not be long and that no one would come to check their tickets.

The air was growing thick quickly with too many bodies and too little ventilation, and though the American landscape flashed past at dizzying speed outside, every minute inside felt like an eternity.

When the train finally arrived in Pittsburgh, Anna was relieved. But once she got off the train, she found herself in a bleak temporary depot. This austere space was a far cry from the splendor of New York.

Dear Reader, the Pittsburgh train station was a reminder that not all was fair and good in the New World. America was both a land of opportunity and a harsh battleground for survival.

Twenty years earlier, in 1877, Pittsburgh had been engulfed in chaos during the Great Railroad Strike. The original station went up in flames as workers, pushed to their breaking point by grueling hours and meager pay, had finally risen. Many innocent lives were lost.

Now, Anna and her children were arriving in this bleak world with nowhere to go and without a single penny. Anna spent her first night in America in that poorly lit, empty depot, her little ones sleeping on either side of her lap. She didn't dare to close her eyes even for a moment. She had to guard her precious children. The family's fate was in her hands.

As the first light of dawn crept through the hall's windows, Anna felt exhausted but resolute. Looking at the scrap of paper with Juraj's address scribbled on it. She was ready to continue the journey to Duquesne.

Fortune Favors the Bold
PITTSBURGH, JULY 1896

The morning crowds surged through the depot, and the striking young woman accompanied by two children drew curious glances from the locals. The Americans couldn't help but admire Anna's high cheekbones, thick mane of golden locks, and delicate silhouette. The weariness did nothing to diminish Anna's etheric beauty.

Perhaps they couldn't look away because they recognized the story etched into her face—a story that echoed in their own family histories. The response was swift and heartfelt.

A horse-drawn carriage was arranged to take the weary travelers to the mine. A basket filled with food—fresh bread, fruit, cheese, and sausage—was thrust into Anna's hands. Someone, perhaps remembering their own arrival as a child, even added toys: a doll for Marienka and a hand-carved wooden boat for Jakub.

Overwhelmed by the unexpected kindness, Anna wept tears of relief. Not even in her most optimistic dreams had she hoped for such a display of genuine hospitality and generosity.

But her joy was short-lived. An unpleasant surprise awaited in Duquesne.

"Mr. Sobota no longer works here," the hard-faced woman in charge told her. "He moved out of the company housing months ago." This administrator made it clear that she had little sympathy for another destitute immigrant family.

Anna was crushed. The hope she had clung to throughout the long and arduous journey across the ocean was gone, and the dream was crumbling before her very eyes.

A Polish miner who had translated the heartbreaking news followed Anna out of the office, his weathered face frowning with concern. Though his compassionate words couldn't soften the blow, he offered what help he could—directions to the Slovak church in the center of Pittsburgh and train tickets for the Duquesne Incline.

He couldn't bear the thought of Anna struggling down Coal Hill's treacherous slope with two children in tow.

Dear Reader, in a land where everyone is foreign, strangers become kin. The small gesture was a reminder that there was still goodness in the world. But alas, the tram did not go all the way. The young mother was now marching through Pittsburgh's bustling streets alone, as her children's sobs grew louder with each step.

Hungry and frightened, their cries reflected Anna's growing despair. They had no money, no shelter, and no Juraj to take care of them.

Carrying the eight-year-old Mária in her arms for the last stretch of the road did not make things easier. Anna's head throbbed, and by the time they reached the church gate, her legs were wobbling.

As she pushed through the heavy wooden doors, a wave of comfort washed over her.

Sanctuary, at last.

Refuge in the Storm

PENNSYLVANIA, JULY 1896

Inside the church, Anna finally let go. She sank to her knees before the statue of the Holy Mother, her fingers trembling as she lit a candle.

The familiar scent of beeswax and incense comforted her troubled mind, and for a moment, she could almost imagine herself back in their village church in Slovakia.

The young woman was so lost in her desperate prayer that she didn't hear the approaching footsteps. Only when a gentle voice interrupted the silence of her reverence did she realize that she was not alone.

"Sister, may I help you?"

Startled, Anna turned around to find a priest standing there watching her with kind eyes.

"*Ako ti môžem pomôcť, sestra?*" he repeated, his compassionate voice carrying the lilt of their homeland.

Anna stood bewildered, hardly believing her ears. Had this priest really spoken to her in Slovak, or was she hallucinating? Could it be that she found a kindred spirit in this foreign and lonely world?

Her head spun trying to make sense of it all. The priest, noticing her unsteadiness, helped her to a nearby pew. Then he disappeared, returning just moments later with two red apples for Jakubko and Marienka and a glass of cool water for their mother.

Whether it was the heavens answering her prayers or simply another serendipitous encounter, Anna stumbled into the warm, caring embrace of the local Slovak community. No longer strangers in a strange land, she and her children were welcomed by fellow immigrants who understood their ordeal.

Anna learned from the priest that Juraj had found work at Carnegie's steel mill, where the pay was better but the dangers no less real. The news of his whereabouts, however, came wrapped in darker tidings.

After the tragedy that had claimed his friend's life, Juraj had lost his way. He had withdrawn from the community that once gave him strength and had sought solace at the bottom of a bottle. For months, all that remained of him were whispered fragments—tales of Juraj's drunken escapades drifted through Pittsburgh.

"The loss broke his spirit," the priest explained, speaking with a heavy heart.

He had witnessed this story too many times—proud men arriving in America full of hope yet becoming trapped in the snares of the many temptations that the New World offered. Their country of origin didn't matter. Slovaks, Poles, Italians, and Irish all drowned their sorrows in alcohol. For some, it was loneliness; for others, the challenge of poverty. Juraj had been pushed over the edge by his grief.

Anna was very quickly learning the dark side of the American Dream.

For every story of success, there were dozens of tales of spirits broken and dreams crushed by exploitation and disillusionment.

As Anna listened to the priest, her determination only grew stronger. This would not be her family's story. She would find her cherished husband and heal his wounded soul with the power of her love.

In America's Little Slovakia everyone knew everyone else, and, much like in the Slovak countryside, any news traveled fast. The tale of the beautiful young wife searching for her lost husband with their two young children, became the talk of every kitchen and street corner.

Would she be able to save him? That question was the topic of every conversation.

The community rallied around the new arrival, everyone offering whatever they could—a change of clothes, a corner to sleep in, a warm meal. Though she was weary after her journey, Anna felt she couldn't rest until she'd found Juraj. As night fell, the young woman left her children safely in the care of some new friends and made her way to the Carnegie Mill.

The streets were alive with strange sounds and bizarre sights, but Anna was indifferent to it all. She had only one thing on her mind—reuniting her family.

When she reached the towering gates of the steelworks, she caught her breath. Her heart raced as she searched for her beloved among the tired men coming and leaving their shifts. She was just a step away from the moment she had dreamed of for nearly two long years.

Anna wondered, "How much could America have changed him?"

A great deal, in fact, yet she knew it was Juraj even before she even saw his face. His head was slumped forward, and his shoulders were heavy with unseen weight.

As she looked at him, the priest's words echoed in her mind. She could hardly recognize the vibrant, dream-filled husband she once knew in this hollow-eyed stranger who was now standing before her.

His eyes, once bright with hope and mischief, now stared blankly ahead, dull and lifeless, as if whatever light had once lived within him had quietly gone out. Seeing him in this state terrified Anna.

"Juraj?" she whispered, her voice trembling from fear and longing.

At the sound of his name, the man halted. Turning, he found himself facing an impossible vision.

In the light of a streetlamp stood a woman dressed in *kroj*. The intricate embroidery of her clothes stood out vividly against the grey, smoke-filled surroundings. Somewhere on the way to America, she lost the headscarf that married women traditionally wore in Slovakia, and her exposed golden locks now glistened in the soft light.

Her eyes, filled with love and quiet compassion, locked onto Juraj's vacant stare, cutting through the layers of numbness he had so carefully built through drink.

Overwhelmed, he rubbed his eyes in disbelief, convinced this had to be another whiskey-induced mirage. What would his wife be doing in this hell? Yet the sight of her blushing cheeks stirred something deep within him, something he'd tried desperately to drown with alcohol. It was too much. Too real. Too close.

He spun away, heart pounding, desperate to escape. He needed another drink and fast.

But her sweet voice followed him: "Ďurko, here I am, *láska moja*.[16] We have come to find you."

Like a balm to his soul, the words spoken in their mother tongue washed over him. Could it really be his darling Anna?

---

16 My love

Reunited

PITTSBURGH, SUMMER 1896

In time, Juraj's bruised mind and heart began to heal in the glow of being reunited with his family. After nearly two long years apart, the Sobotas were together again.

Supported by his wife and two children, Juraj clawed his way back from the grip of drink. Achieving sobriety was no small feat; many never broke free from alcohol. In Slovak neighborhoods across the country, good men were swallowed by the plague of alcoholism that haunted so many immigrant families.

For Juraj, a spark grew in his heart, giving him the strength to overcome his addiction and to build a better future for them all.

But once his family had come, life wasn't just about work anymore. Now, it was about sharing moments, creating memories, and introducing the ones he loved to the wonders of their adopted homeland. America held marvels they could never have imagined in their village in Slovakia.

There was so much to do to make up for the lost time!

One sun-drenched afternoon, Juraj took his son to a Pittsburgh Pirates baseball game. The stadium buzzed with

excitement—the sharp crack of the bat echoed through the air, the crowd roared with every hit, and the green expanse of the field stretched before them.

For a few precious hours, father and son were no longer immigrants—they were simply part of the American moment, cheering their team on, sitting side by side in the sun.

Jakub was mesmerized by this spectacle. Perched on the edge of his seat, eyes wide with wonder, he felt like he was on top of the world. He didn't notice his father's sadness. It was there, though—woven into Juraj's voice as he patiently explained the rules of the game.

This was Juraj's first baseball game since Michal's passing, and the poignant memories came flooding back—the two of them sharing roasted peanuts, Michal explaining the rules between innings, his friend's warm laughter rolling through the stands louder than any cheer.

The rawness of Juraj's grief had softened with time, but the ache remained. Michal's death had carved a quiet void in his friend's heart. Now, enjoying his son's amazement—so much like his own the first time he had come with Michal—Juraj felt his friend's spirit stir inside him. In Jakub's wide-eyed wonder, something of Michal lived on.

As the crowd erupted around them, Juraj shed a quiet tear. He raised his cup and took a slow sip of Coca-Cola. "This one's for you, brother," he whispered.

Marienka was also treated to an extraordinary experience.

She couldn't sleep for days when her daddy told her that the circus was coming to town—and not just any circus!

The Barnum & Bailey show was the most renowned traveling circus in all of America. It was a whirl of blazing lights, thunderous music, exotic animals, and acrobats who seemed to defy the laws of gravity with each daring leap.

Mária was transfixed by the enthralling performance before her. She clapped her small hands with such fervor that they grew red and tender.

Juraj's heart melted at her awe and her pure, unrestrained joy.

But it was Anna who brought out the deepest feelings in Juraj.

Anna was more than his wife. She was his North Star, his inspiration, his daily reminder that love could cross oceans to rescue a lost man back from the very precipice of hell.

One day, he noticed Anna's lingering gaze on a dress displayed in the window of Braddock's finest shop. She looked just a moment too long, then quickly turned away, careful not to dwell on a wish for something so clearly beyond their means.

The very next day, he returned and bought it.

This dress, which was styled in the latest American fashion, transformed Anna into the embodiment of metropolitan elegance, though Juraj would argue she had always possessed that grace. The fine fabric clung to her slender frame as if it had been waiting in that window just for her.

On Sunday afternoons, when the couple promenaded through their neighborhood, she wore her new dress with quiet dignity. Other women paused their conversations, as eyes followed her with whispers of admiration. Gentlemen tipped their hats in respect to the striking woman who moved with such poise.

Watching her, Juraj's heart swelled with pride and gratitude.

America was changing them, but it was also bringing out something that had always lived within them—strength, and the courage to become more than their circumstances had once allowed.

As Anna walked beside him on the streets of Pittsburgh, looking so beautiful and dignified, Juraj knew that every callus on his hands, every long hour at the mill, was worth it.

Making Pittsburgh Home
SUMMER 1896

In the late 19th century, Pittsburgh was a bustling patchwork of ethnic neighborhoods.

Among the narrow streets and humble homes, hundreds of thousands of Slavs created new lives for themselves, building tight-knit communities that allowed them to preserve the languages and traditions of their former countries.

Churches became their sanctuaries, social clubs their gathering places, and cultural events the highlight of the annual calendar.

A Little Slovakia blossomed around the Catholic Church of St. Elizabeth. More than merely a house of worship, it was the community's spiritual oasis.

Here, immigrants could unburden their souls to a priest who understood their native language. And here, they could find support in a like-minded community that shared their struggles, hopes, and roots.

There was also a Slovak doctor, a Slovak hairdresser, a Slovak butcher, and a Slovak grocery store that stocked ingredients from home—paprika, caraway seeds, and more.

Everywhere they went, the Sobotas were surrounded by the familiar sounds of their native tongue, which was also why Anna never mastered English.

In this microcosm of their homeland, the family found a new rhythm.

The price of their newfound hope had been Anna's ruby locket—a treasured heirloom that had been passed down through at least five generations of Slovak women, from mother to daughter, with each successive owner guarding it like a sacred thread of their lineage.

The loss still stung. But when she watched Juraj leave each morning with his lunch pail and saw the children's cheeks grow fuller by the week, Anna was reminded that meaningful sacrifice plants seeds not to slake today's hunger but to generate tomorrow's harvest.

Occasionally, her mind drifted to the looming debt to the tavern owner, but she pushed such thoughts away. She couldn't worry about it now when everything else felt so right.

With Juraj spending dawn to dusk at the mill, Anna ventured into the New World, eager to explore its perks and opportunities.

She was pleased to discover that sugar was much cheaper in America than in Upper Hungary where it was still an unattainable luxury. Anna used to sweeten her cakes with honey, which was still far too precious to waste on everyday treats. But in Pittsburgh, she could bake *koláče*[17]

---

17 Cakes

filled with poppy seeds, nuts, or tart plum jam every week, making the sweetness of their new life quite literal.

Meat, once a rare indulgence only enjoyed on a handful of Sundays, could now grace the Sobota dining table several times a week. A simple roast chicken, a slice of beef, or pork stuffing were an undeniable proof that America, harsh as it could be, offered possibilities unimaginable for people like them.

However, the indisputed king of their weekly menus was the Friday night *holúbky*. In Krivany, this special dish was served only for weddings or other grand occasions. In America, Anna could make it as often as she wanted, and so she did!

The cabbage leaves, tenderly wrapped around seasoned meat and rice, had always been Juraj's favorite. Anna knew it was more than just a meal to her husband. Each bite evoked memories of happy times with his parents, their native village, and Anna and Juraj's very own wedding day.

On Fridays, knowing there would be *holúbky*, Juraj always rushed home from the mill, impatient to savor the familiar flavors of the homeland.

Holúbky were legendary not just in the Sobota family, but throughout the Slovak community. Anna particularly admired Mrs. Javorová, a fellow immigrant from eastern Slovakia, who had transformed her family recipe into a thriving empire.

Initially, Anna felt intimidated by this hard-working, quick-witted, and fiercely independent matriarch. Over time, however, she grew captivated by the older woman's entrepreneurial spirit.

Anna was learning that in America, women could be more than wives and mothers; they could be business owners, decision-makers, respected voices in the community. Some, like Mrs. Javorová, were even earning more than their husbands.

While Anna searched for her own place in this new and ever-shifting world, she turned these possibilities over in her mind while kneading dough and washing dishes in their cramped, Pittsburgh apartment. Could she one day step into such a role herself? Perhaps, but for now, she found quiet satisfaction in the familiar rhythms of being wife and mother.

Anna took nothing for granted. Every morning, she counted her blessings. Being reunited with Juraj, having a full pantry and a roof over their heads.

"If only the roof were a little sturdier," she noted.

The new company-allocated family dwelling next to the Edgar Thomson Steel Works was a testament to the industrial age's stark efficiency. Built to house as many workers as possible at the lowest possible cost, endless rows of identical wooden shacks stretched toward the smoky Pittsburgh horizon. It challenged even Anna's modest expectations.

The house was barely big enough for a family of four, and the walls were so thin they trembled with each turn of the nearby mill's relentless gears. A crooked outhouse and a tiny kitchen shared with three other immigrant families were a source of daily frustration.

But it was still a thousand times better than going to bed alone.

Between Two Worlds

AUTUMN 1896

Having found their footing at last, the Sobota parents turned their attention to the opportunities America offered their offspring. Like other Slovak parents in America at the time, Anna and Juraj were caught in a dilemma.

How could they nurture their children's American future without sacrificing their Slovak identity?

Navigating the demands of the New World while remaining connected to the old one was a fine balance to maintain, and language became the most delicate battlefield.

Even in Pittsburgh's Slavic neighborhoods, where the language of the Old Country sounded from every doorway, English inevitably crept into immigrant homes.

Jakubko and Mária attended an American school, where only English was spoken. They used English on the streets when playing with their non-Slovak friends. Slovak Sunday school at St. Elizabeth's couldn't compete with five full days of American schooling.

It was only natural that the two children began to blend English words into their Slovak conversations at home with their parents. Juraj and Anna were taken aback by how quickly their children were adapting.

"This never happened with Hungarian!" Juraj exclaimed in disbelief. Back home, stern-faced teachers had spared no effort in trying to force Slovak children to learn Hungarian. But no matter how hard they tried, the children's minds remained closed to the language.

Yet, here in America, the children were keen to learn and use the English language and all the customs that were not their own, moving between the two worlds with ease.

Juraj and Anna observed this transformation with hearts that were divided. Each English word that rolled from their children's tongues was a tiny grain of their heritage slipping away. And every Slovak word spoken during play felt like a small victory against the rising tide of change.

Women are most especially the keepers of cultural identity and traditions, and so Anna felt the weight of this responsibility quite heavily.

As much as she wanted her children to master English, she never wanted them to forget they were Slovak. And so, she quietly appointed herself the guardian of her family's Slovak soul.

Within the sanctuary of their home, Anna declared, only the language of their forefathers would be spoken.

"Let America claim the world beyond these walls," she told her children firmly, "but here, the old ways will endure."

Slovakia might have been thousands of miles away, but it was and would always be their homeland.

Smog, Dirt and Wickedness
WINTER 1896

Although life in Little Slovakia offered the Sobotas many conveniences and much excitement, deep in their bones, both Juraj and Anna felt that something was wrong.

America's benefits, they discovered, came at a high price.

To begin with, living in America was expensive. Juraj's steel mill wage, which was abundant when his family was still in Upper Hungary, barely sustained the four of them in Pittsburgh. The children's schooling also strained the family's purse, and their debt to the innkeeper cast a dark shadow even across the Atlantic.

Unwilling to lose their ancestral home in Krivany, Juraj and Anna struck a desperate bargain with a local moneylender just before the one-year contract was about to expire.

Anna was deeply grateful when Juraj managed to secure the arrangement in the final hours. She couldn't imagine allowing the home built by the hard work of her father to fall into the hands of the greedy innkeeper. Besides, though they seldom spoke of it aloud, the Sobotas carried a quiet, steadfast belief that one day, they would return home.

But as one problem was solved, another, more daunting, took its place. That was the fate of immigrants: a constant trade between hope and hardship.

The pressure of the enlarged debt drove Juraj to take on more hours at the mill. His grinding schedule of twelve-hour shifts six days a week left little room for additional labor. Not knowing what else to do, he volunteered for Sunday work as well, surrendering his only day of rest, the comfort of church, and precious time with his wife and children.

Husband and wife became like strangers sharing a roof. When Juraj wasn't working in the mill, he was sleeping—too exhausted for more than a few mumbled words to Anna. Their family life was crumbling into fleeting moments and hurried exchanges in the grey hours between work and sleep. There was no time for Sunday strolls, rest, or play with the kids.

This miserable existence stood in stark contrast to the prosperous future that the Sobotas had envisioned for themselves when Juraj first sailed for America.

Eventually, the novelty of cheap meat and sugar wore off as well. What good were American dollars in their pockets when they came at the cost of their time, health, and togetherness of the family?

More and more, their thoughts turned to the homestead in Krivany, the one they had once dreamed of expanding into a farm. Now that they were living empty lives in Pittsburgh, that ambition seemed distant, almost unreachable.

The promise of America felt more like a burden than a blessing.

Anna had to wonder, "Does the life we live justify the sacrifices we had to make to get here?"

Try as she might to console herself with the memories of her favorite wildflowers, the burgeoning streams, and the vibrant forests of home, sweet recollections made the grimness of their current reality only more unbearable.

There seemed to be no escape from it.

Greyness seeped into every corner of their existence—both tangible and spiritual. On some days, Anna had to keep the windows shut to prevent the omnipresent dust from covering the floors, the bedding, the dishes... everything! Even the tomatoes she so painstakingly grew in the tiny plot of land behind their house wilted. Yet, the physical pollution was nothing compared to the moral decay she witnessed.

Pittsburgh was a chaotic swirl of temptation and deceit. The city's streets teemed with vice and wickedness. Anna despised the saloons lining nearly every block near the mill. Even worse were the seedy gambling dens and brothels lying in wait for lonely workers at the end of their long shifts.

"America provides as many ways to lose money as to earn it," she said to Juraj. Her heart ached at the thought of their children being surrounded by such corruption.

But nothing tormented Anna more than Juraj's backbreaking job.

Hour after endless hour, he worked with dangerous machinery in insufferable heat. All it would take was one moment of distraction—a slip of the hand, a misplaced step—and Juraj could easily scorch his face, lose his arm, or worse.

"And for what?" Anna lamented to her neighbor. "Our family barely makes ends meet."

This wise woman was a sought-after matchmaker and arbitrator of neighborhood disputes. She patiently listened to Anna's frustrations. With a gentle nod, she encouraged Anna to speak to her husband about it, but Anna didn't dare.

Days passed. Anna's sadness grew heavy; her patience thinned.

One evening, after serving Juraj his favorite meal, her fear cracked open, and she burst into tears.

"Juraj, *láska moja*,"[18] she said between sobs. "There must be another way for us."

---

18 My love

Out of the Furnace
SPRING 1897

At the end of the 19th century, Pittsburgh offered new immigrants two choices—the infernal furnaces of the steel mills or the hungry depths of the coal mines. Having endured both, the Sobota family stood at the edge of a momentous decision.

Should they go back to Upper Hungary? If they did, of course, their return wouldn't be the glorious homecoming Juraj had once envisaged.

Instead of returning as a triumphant *amerikáni*[19], the family would crawl home as defeated and debt-ridden peasants, even poorer than they'd been when they left!

Their American odyssey would turn to ash. Gone would be the golden promise of saving one thousand US dollars. Gone, too, would be the vision of new land, new livestock, and a bigger home.

Night after night, Juraj and Anna lay sleepless, trapped in an impossible predicament in which they were torn

---

19 Slovaks who had returned to their homeland from America

between pride and desperation. Had they truly squandered their one chance at a decent life?

Then came the flyer.

Tucked among forgotten papers at the back of the church, a yellowed pamphlet caught Juraj's eye. It proclaimed, *"Návrat k vidieku"* (Return to the Farm.) The three Slovak words nearly leaped off the page, promising something almost too good to be true.

The pamphlet was from the Slovak Colonization Company, an organization Juraj remembered hearing about. It had been founded two years before his arrival by a small group of men who were deeply concerned about the future of Slovaks in America. Their vision was bold and simple—they wanted to help their compatriots reclaim a pastoral existence but on American soil.

When Juraj first arrived in America his heart had been set on a triumphant return to Slovakia, and so he had ignored the meetings this group held in the church basement. The idea of settling on an American farm was of no interest to a man dreaming of his homeland.

But necessity, Dear Reader, has a way of opening a person's eyes to fresh possibilities.

The Slovak Colonization Company had been a great success. Dozens of Slovak families had left the Smoky City behind to begin new lives on the plains of Arkansas. These Slovak immigrants had traded the industrial wasteland for the promise of a wholesome rural life in the American South.

By the time Juraj noticed this old pamphlet, he had been worn to the bone by the grind of industrial life. He slipped the flyer into his coat pocket, and something stirred deep inside him—just as he had been touched on that fateful day when he first heard of the American emperor with his streets paved in gold.

Representatives of the Slovak Colonization Company—known by its supporters as the Company—spoke of the Slovak pioneers in Arkansas with pride. Their tales painted a vivid picture of the men and women who had rediscovered their dignity and purpose. No longer mere cogs in the unforgiving industrial machine, these brave Slovak families had become masters of their own destinies.

Could this be the way forward for the Sobotas? Could they "return to the farm" and remain in America?

PART 4

BACK TO ROOTS

Great Rewards Require Great Sacrifices

ARKANSAS, SPRING 1897

Juraj's meager earnings from the mills in Pittsburgh quickly brought him back to reality. Their savings, squeezed from countless hours of toil, would cover only half the cost of the Arkansas land.

If his family wanted to seize the opportunity to leave Pittsburgh, Juraj would have to return to Pennsylvania's industrial hell, while Anna and the children pioneered on their prairie homestead alone.

The prospect of another separation filled Anna with dread. Yet the price of hope, it seemed, always involved a parting.

This time it would be different—and even harder than before. She would have to fend for herself and the children in the vast, unfamiliar expanse of the Grand Prairie, far from the close-knit village community of Krivany, where neighbors were like family and help was always within reach.

She was worried. Who would be there when she needed aid? Was this a risk worth taking?

But under Pittspurgh's perpetual haze, factory fumes dimmed even the brightest of sunny days. And the ceaseless rattle of industry drowned out any sense of peace. Amidst all of this, one thing became painfully clear to the Sobota family—they would not find happiness in the Steel City.

Day by day, the primordial call of the land grew stronger until, finally, it surpassed the worst of their fears.

It was the spring of 1897 when the Sobota family arrived in Slovaktown, Arkansas, joining thirty other families on three hundred acres of untamed prairie. This was the only town in America named after their beloved homeland—clearly, a good omen.

Yet, Dear Reader, their trials and tribulations were far from over.

As Juraj and Anna walked hand in hand toward their plot of newly purchased land, their hearts fluttered with anticipation. They held their breath—ready and eager to work hard, to finally build the life they had always dreamed of.

But what they saw before them was not fertile farmland. It was wild, windswept prairie—a grassland that was covered by an impenetrable sea of seven-foot-tall and deeply rooted prairie grass.

Juraj and Anna looked at each other, each of them understanding that this was to be a test of their faith. If they could remain steadfast, God's reward would be generous.

Still, it took every ounce of courage and strength not to turn around and run in some other direction.

They had no proper house to live in, so the Sobotas made their home in the barn of a generous neighbor. Anna fashioned their beds from the abundant prairie grass that covered their land, trying her best to give the children a sense of comfort through what was yet another dramatic uprooting of their lives. As a mother, she knew that even a semblance of a home—no matter how humble it might be—would make facing the unknown a little easier for her children.

Thankfully, Jakub and Mária were excited by the transition, rather than terrified by it.

And the barn, though rough and uncomfortable, would have to do for now as their lodging. Juraj would build a proper home for his family later, with the help of their new community, but he couldn't give his attention to that issue now.

Each passing day was further depleting their precious saving, and Juraj had to confront the most pressing challenge initially: how to feed his family while transforming the prairie into arable farmland.

It was obvious that the vast and untamed Arkansan landscape would offer no quick harvest to sustain them. The prairie, with its defiant grass and stubborn soil, seemed determined to defy them at every turn.

However, the Slovaks had survived generations of hardship in their own homeland, and from this they had learned the art of resourcefulness.

Rather than wasting their scant time and money on futile experiments, the Sobotas learned from the earlier

settlers of Slovaktown, who had already begun to unlock the prairie's secrets.

The towering seven-foot-tall prairie grass, which first appeared to be an insurmountable obstacle, ultimately revealed itself as an unexpected blessing. In the future, it became fodder for farm animals.

Taming the Prairie
ARKANSAS AND PITTSBURGH, SUMMER / AUTUMN 1897

Week after week, Juraj and Anna wrestled the unyielding land into submission. Their scythes glinted in the sun as they swung in continuous arcs, battling the obstinate prairie grass, one blade at a time. The work bent their backs and bloodied their hands, but the harvested hay brought precious dollars while they slowly transformed wilderness into farmland.

But nature was a harsh mistress. As spring gave way to the scorching heat of an Arkansan summer, the prairie grass turned from obstacle to a potential threat. The grass became so dry and brittle that a single lightning strike or a stray spark could have ignited an inferno that would consume everything in its path.

The strong prairie winds carried a foreboding peril—the winds could drive fires across the open landscape with terrifying speed and fury. This unstoppable force would at times claim homes, harvests, livestock… and souls.

Each year brought new tragedies.

Slovaktown was not spared. Just the summer before the Sobotas arrived, a neighbor's six-year-old daughter had been trapped in her family's home and was suffocated during an uncontrollable burst of wind and fire.

This savage frontier bore little resemblance to the gentle, pastoral landscapes of their European homeland. Gone were the soft, rolling green hills dotted with small family farmsteads and thick Carpathian forests. This was an indifferent flatland that tested the pioneers' resolve with each dawn and with every passing season.

Many a woman, left alone on the windswept prairie, lost her mind to the isolation and endless hardships. It burdened Anna, too. Tragic tales gripped Anna with a visceral, maternal terror. After Juraj returned to Pittsburgh—working to earn the rest of the money needed to pay for the land—Anna would lay awake for nights on end, imagining what horrors might befall her own children.

In those trying and lonely times, Anna was driven less by dreams of prosperity than by a cold fear of what might go wrong. The young woman was propelled to work with a desperate, almost inhuman, intensity. Anna was consumed by a single, fierce purpose: to tame this menacing wilderness before it could harm Jakub and Mária.

Each sunset found her hands raw with bleeding blisters, her shoulders and neck burned crimson by the merciless sun. Yet, each morning she rose again, tying a scarf over her head and tightening the apron around her diminishing waistline.

The hard labor stripped away her flesh but never her will.

What she endured might have broken a weaker soul, but Anna was strengthened by an unyielding determination that many mothers know.

Meanwhile, for Juraj, life in Pittsburgh was difficult in other ways.

Juraj's world had narrowed to a single purpose. Now, he barely noticed the steel mill's infernal conditions. He worked seven days a week, counting the time until he could be with his family once again.

Yet something darker than the usual fog haunted Pittsburgh's smoky streets. Industrial America was simmering with workers' rage, and that fall—while Juraj was in Pittsburgh—the pot boiled over.

Tensions between the miners and mine owners escalated near Hazleton, Pennsylvania, in September 1897, culminating in one of the bloodiest chapters in American labor history. What began as a peaceful strike ended in a massacre when the sheriff's deputies opened fire on unarmed protesters.

Nineteen workers, including several Slovaks, were killed instantly, and dozens more were seriously wounded. The tragedy sent shockwaves through the immigrant communities across Pennsylvania and dominated Slovak-American newspapers for weeks.

When Juraj heard about the massacre, he knew he had to work faster. He stretched his shifts whenever possible, driving his body to the limits and placing his very life at risk so that he would be able to leave Pittsburgh as quickly as possible.

Every dollar he earned carried him one step closer to escaping this industrial powder keg.

Together at Last
JANUARY 1898

Once Juraj returned to Arkansas, his family's fortunes began to shift, and life took a turn for the better.

To her great surprise, Anna discovered she was pregnant again!

Haunted by the memory of her last complicated childbirth in Krivany, she kept the happy news to herself for as long as she could. Her fingers often traced the subtle curve of her belly, as the midwife's words echoed in her mind: "You and the baby are lucky to be alive, but you will never again conceive another child, my dear."

When she could no longer hide her growing belly, she decided to leave the past behind.

God had held her before, and Anna entrusted her worries to His will once again. When Juraj found out that another child was coming, he was ecstatic! So were Jakub and Mária, and their joy soon rippled through the entire community, as everyone waited for this new arrival in eager anticipation.

A healthy baby boy was born on Christmas Eve of 1898. His parents named him Adam—the first American-born Slovak in the Sobota family line.

The baptism, which took place early in the next year, was a celebration for the Sobotas and for everyone in Slovaktown. This was before the local Catholic church was built, and so the christening took place in a neighbor's barn, whose beams had been festooned with ribbons by loving hands. The barn was transformed beyond recognition to honor the occasion.

The whole community came to welcome dashing baby Adam. *Slivovica* flowed freely, and trays of *koláče* kept the christening party going long into the night. The arrival of a new generation was an unmistakable sign that Slovak roots were being firmly planted in the New World.

These children, bearing the surnames of their Slovak ancestors, represented more than the continuation of a family line. They were a living testament to their predecessors' resilience, courage, and strength to transplant their lives to a new land. In the young children's innocent faces, the hardworking farmers of Slovaktown saw the promise of legacy.

Seeds of Providence

ARKANSAS, EARLY 1900s

Slovaktown flourished through the tenacity of its residents.

The gardens tended by the women yielded fruits and vegetables that sustained their families through every season of the year. Their green thumbs yielded more than their families needed, and so the surplus harvest found its way to the marketplace in Stuttgart, Arkansas, where earlier German immigrants had built a thriving economy.

The men of Slovaktown tended to the growing flocks and herds, and traded prairie hay along the railroad tracks. As they cleared the land of wild grass and opened the earth, the once forbidding frontier began to look like a home. The future seemed bright.

In the spring of 1899, Juraj joined his neighbors for the first time in sowing their fields—imagining golden stretches of wheat stretching as far as the eye could see.

At last, it felt like the time had come to capitalize on the promise of America—a land that rewarded men who worked hard and dreamed big.

But nature had other plans.

The Arkansan fields flooded that season, leaving behind rotting crops and crushed hopes.

The Grand Prairie had a heavy clay base and a thin layer of topsoil, and this posed an unexpected challenge for the families of Slovaktown.

Season after season, the farmers planted the crops they knew from their homeland, determined to reap a bountiful harvest. When wheat withered, they tried barley. When that failed, they resorted to hardy rye.

The soil, however, remained indifferent to their ambition. Again and again, floods came without warning, washing away months of careful cultivation in mere moments. The farmers' efforts were in vain, and Slovaktown teetered on the brink of ruin.

And, so, they turned to prayer.

In 1900, the Church of Saints Cyril and Methodius, built and funded by the good people of the community, was consecrated. This house of worship stood as a powerful symbol of their uncompromising faith.

Yet, even as they knelt in fervent prayer, pleading for divine intervention, under the watchful gaze of the Byzantine saints that brought Christianity into the Slavic world, their fields continued to be barren.

The blessings they so desperately sought did not come. Had the patron saints abandoned their children in this foreign land?

It seemed that all was lost until in the fateful year of 1904 a stroke of genius—or perhaps divine inspiration—transformed everything.

Whether it was the saint's whispered guidance or a spark of human ingenuity, the discovery was made of one unlikely crop that would go on to salvage the town forever. Rice.

With the sense that they had nothing left to lose, the Sobotas and their neighbors plunged their all into this final gamble. To their great surprise, the clay soil that had mocked their earlier crops and their traditional farming methods suddenly yielded a bounty beyond the wildest of their dreams. Rice emerged from their stubborn fields like an answer to their prayers.

Almost overnight, this collection of struggling homesteads became a thriving farm town, its roots deepening and strengthening with each passing season.

A Slovak schoolhouse rose from the prairie, its walls echoing with the voices of children speaking their parents' native tongue.

Soon the schoolhouse was followed by a Slovak shop, which spared Juraj the long wagon rides to Stuttgart for provisions.

With rice, everyone in Slovaktown thrived. Sometimes Juraj had to pinch himself; he hardly believed their good fortune.

The hardships that he and his family had endured during their early American years seemed like a lifetime ago.

There was, however, one bleak memory that remained forever seared into Juraj's mind: Michal's tragic death in the darkness of Coal Hill.

To honor his friend's sacrifice and untimely death, Juraj and his sons, Jakub and Adam, erected a memorial on their land. The hand-carved stone was a witness to the price paid by early Slovak immigrants, its inscription a lasting reminder to future generations of the strength of these pioneers.

Within a few short years of settling on the plains of Arkansas, the Sobota family's dream of having successful farms became a reality—not in the Old Country, as they'd once imagined, but here, in the New World.

Still, their hearts continued to long for *slovenská zem*, the Slovak land.

Shadow over the Homeland
KINGDOM OF HUNGARY, EARLY 1900s

More than a decade had passed since Juraj and Anna had left Slovakia, and they missed Krivany dearly. But as the years went by, they spoke less and less of returning. And then one day, they stopped speaking of it altogether.

Troubling news began to arrive in letters from the Old Country. The Kingdom of Hungary was transforming, and not for the better.

It seemed that the government's *magyarization* agenda was growing in ferocity. Hell-bent on forging a single national identity, the authorities were determined to assimilate the Kingdom's diverse peoples so that they would all think of themselves as Hungarians. The authorities were relentless in finding new ways of penetrating the Slovak world.

They tempted Slovaks to *magyarize* their names to climb the social ladder. They infiltrated Slovak churches and appointed Magyar priests.

Tensions rippled through Slovak villages as families faced an impossible choice: surrender their identity or risk punishment.

The rich cultural tapestry that had been the Kingdom's hallmark for centuries was being unraveled in the name of cultural unity.

All of this came together in a heartbreaking massacre that took place in 1907 in the Slovak village of Černová. When Juraj and Anna heard about this tragedy, they considered themselves fortunate to be in America, where freedom of expression was not just a privilege but the birthright of every human being.

Dear Reader, bear with us as we recount the dreadful event.

In 1907, Černová had become a symbol of the cultural plight facing ethnic minorities across the Kingdom of Hungary. In this small Slovak village, hardworking residents had pooled their humble savings to build a new Catholic church, a long-held dream shared by most devout communities.

The good people of Černová wanted a priest of their own culture to consecrate their church on its grand unveiling. The man they chose was none other than the celebrated Father Andrej Hlinka.

Father Hlinka was a fierce defender of Slovak rights and a thunderous voice against the ongoing cultural oppression by the Magyars—a hero, in other words, to the Slovak people. His sermons burned with the fire of national pride and with unbending resistance. He always empowered his parishioners to stand strong and proud—as Slovaks.

But when the people of Černová gathered for this momentous day, what was meant to be a celebration turned into a catastrophe. On the day of the consecration, Father Hlinka was conspicuously absent. In his place stood a *maďarón*, a Slovak who had renounced his heritage to serve Hungarian interests.

The unwelcome substitute was flanked by armed gendarmes. The message was unmistakable: even in their own house of worship, Slovaks were expected to bow to Magyar authority.

The Christians of Černová could not have such a deplorable symbol of betrayal stand at their own altar. United by this insult to their dignity and enraged by the blatant disregard for their own wishes on this sacred day, the Slovak villagers formed a human blockade to stop the *maďarón* priest from entering the church.

Outnumbered, the gendarmes—many of whom were themselves ethnic Slovaks—opened fire on the unarmed crowd. Fifteen villagers died.

Ultimately, news of this "Slovak incident" reverberated far beyond the village. Thanks to more than two hundred Slovak-American newspapers and magazines, immigrants closely followed the dramatic developments in the Old Country. The tragedy at Černová became a rallying cry that united Slovaks on both sides of the ocean into a single, resolute spirit.

In the industrial cities of the northern U.S., protesters took to the streets. In rural communities like Slovaktown, solidarity took a more practical form: money was collected and sent to Upper Hungary, supporting those who dared to resist the tyranny of *magyarization*.

For Juraj and Anna, the harrowing accounts in the Slovak-American press and the letters from neighbors and family back home reinforced their decision to remain in Arkansas.

They felt there was nothing left for them in Upper Hungary. The grief that Juraj and Anna felt for what was happening in their homeland was matched only by their gratitude for being far away.

Tales of brutal crackdowns, midnight inspections, neighbors turning against each other, and children beaten for speaking their native language felt like dark fairytales to those now living under the protection of American democracy.

What We Brought with Us

ARKANSAS, 1900s

Nostalgia is a loyal companion to immigrants. On long winter evenings far away from polarized political events, the transplanted Slovaks would experience a deep yearning for their homeland. This nostalgia would settle over Slovaktown like the heavy fog that blanketed the Arkansas plains. The longing seeped through closed doors and shuttered windows. It was impossible to keep out.

The settlers found their hearts aching for the familiar rhythms of their old lives, the sights and smells of the places they once loved—the toll of church bells marking the hours, the crunch of snow beneath boots, or the sound of Slovak prayers filling ancient church halls...

Someone would inevitably reach for the *slivovica,* and rounds of shots would circulate, glasses clinking in warm candlelight. As the familiar burn spread through their bodies, the tug-of-war between the yearning to return and the determination to hold on to their American Dream began to soften.

Homeland was here and now, not thousands of miles away.

"*Na zdravie!*"[20] With each sip, tears and bittersweet stories would spill forth: tales of childhood mischief, the rolling hills of Šariš, the memories of harvests and Christmases long past...

For many, the toasts echoed into the night, but Juraj never again took another drink. He had been sober since Anna and the children arrived in America.

In the evenings, however, Juraj and Anna would also find themselves speaking of things they thought they had forgotten: the pink light on the hills above Krivany moments before sunset, the silence of the dense Carpathian forests, the sweet peace of walking beneath the willow trees lining the riverbanks, the sacred shade inside the church where generations of their family had been baptized and married.

Oh, how the two of them pined to step inside this world again, if only for a moment, so that they could breathe in the unmistakable fragrance of centuries of burning beeswax candles and incense.

In America, everything was so new. It wasn't possible to transport the weather-worn stones of Krivany's old village square, or the ancient cemeteries where their ancestors were laid to rest. They had, however, carried something far more precious with them to the New World. They brought the wisdom of their forefathers and the customs and traditions that gave life rhythm and meaning.

In Slovaktown, these treasures that were transported inside the people who came, found fertile soil.

---

20 Cheers!

At community gatherings, when traditional folk songs filled the air, even those who had never seen the Old Country somehow knew the dance steps. The younger generation may have stumbled over pronouncing the Slovak words, but the melodies lived in their blood.

And also, Dear Reader, there was one thing that healed homesickness more than anything else. The food.

In the sacred space of Slovaktown kitchens, a different kind of alchemy took place.

Here, the familiar aromas of simmering *kapusta*,[21] frying onions, and freshly baked bread wove a spell that could transport the heart across thousands of miles and back to the Old Country. Plump *pirohy*, tasty *holúbky*, spicy *klobása*, smoky *slanina*[22], and fragrant *koláče* were more than just mere sustenance.

Making and sharing these foods from the homeland was a delicious act of remembrance, a way to keep the Old Country alive for those who had quietly accepted they might never see it—or might never see it again.

Juraj's smoked *klobása*, which had marked the beginning of the Sobotas' American journey, became the stuff of legend beyond the Grand Prairie. The sausages, made according to a treasured family recipe passed down from his father and his father before him, were cherished far and wide.

The secret lay not only in the blend of spices, but in the stories Juraj shared with anyone who asked—tales of

---

21 Cabbage
22 Bacon

winter pig slaughters in the Old Country, when neighbors gathered at dawn with steaming mugs of tea, snow crunching underfoot as the fire was lit and the work began. Those who listened swore they could taste all of it in every bite. People would travel miles for a taste of proud Slovak tradition, washing down the smoked goods with a shot of fiery *slivovica*.

Anna created her own legacy through her *holúbky*. The succulent pork and rice cabbage rolls were requested at every community gathering, from christenings to weddings and even at funerals. The recipe she shared freely with friends and neighbors was not just a list of ingredients—it was a gift that would be carried forth across generations.

These culinary traditions were planted in the New World like fertile seeds. With more and more Slovak children born in America, and the original settlers laid to rest in American earth, these seeds took root and flowered into something new: a Slovak-American identity.

Roots and Horizons

ARKANSAS, 1910s

The wheel of time kept turning, and prosperity flowed into the Arkansan plains. Deep in the Grand Prairie, Slovak farmers joined forces with Czech settlers in Hazen and German immigrants in Stuttgart. Their combined knowledge, determination, and a shared dream laid the foundation for what would eventually become America's rice-growing heartland.

By the 1910s, what had once been a tiny settlement had transformed into a thriving Slovak community of more than fifty families.

The variety of faiths became their strength—Catholics, Lutherans, and Russian Orthodox believers lived, worked, and prayed side by side. In time, the denominations built their own churches and left behind three cemeteries—a clear memento of the religious diversity of Slovak–America.

While the Sobotas were busy transforming their American dream into reality, much had changed on the other side of the Atlantic.

The First World War shattered Europe's great empires. The thousand-year-old Kingdom of Hungary disappeared from the map like a fading memory, and in its wake came Czechoslovakia—which served as a fragile beacon of hope on a war-ravaged continent.

This vision came to life not only through the sacrifices of those who endured hardship in Central Europe but also through the tireless efforts of American Slovaks and Czechs, who campaigned, petitioned, gave their voices, and often donated the fruits of their labor to the cause of freedom for their ancestral homeland.

To the surprise and elation of many, including Slovak immigrants abroad, the young republic flourished. Under the visionary leadership of President Tomáš Garrigue Masaryk, Czechoslovakia emerged as one of the world's most promising democracies and strongest economies.

Its success beckoned many Slovak emigrants to return and help build their newly liberated homeland.

But not the Sobotas.

Firmly rooted in the Arkansas soil, the Sobota children and descendants felt their future lay not in the country they had left behind but in the one that had welcomed them with open arms.

The Sobota offspring carried the pioneering spirit of their parents further in their own remarkable ways. Jakub and Mária grew into young and ambitious adults who became naturalized American citizens.

They both felt the pull of opportunities beyond the fields of Arkansas and set out to build new lives in the bustling

cities of America's Northeast. Jakub, now known as Jacob, was a dashing young man who established himself as a legal clerk within Chicago's vibrant immigrant community. His marriage to the daughter of a Polish immigrant wove another strand into the rich tapestry of American ethnicity and aspiration.

Mária, who took after her beautiful mother, blazed an extraordinary trail in Cleveland's burgeoning automotive industry. With quiet determination, she rose to become the right hand of the chief executive at the Chandler Motor Car Company, shattering the glass ceilings of what was thought possible for a woman of her time.

Mária married an Irish-American, adding yet another chapter to the family's evolving story. Their three children symbolized the melting pot that America continued to be.

The destiny of Adam, the youngest, was to become the keeper of the family's agricultural heritage.

The only one of the children who was born in America, he took his first wobbly steps in the tiny garden Anna lovingly tended during their early years on the prairie. Adam was raised on the homestead and grew up with its success, so it was little surprise that he felt the call of being a steward of the land most strongly.

While his older siblings sought fortune in distant cities, Adam-like his father—never wished to be anything other than a farmer.

Though raised on the stories of Slovakia, Adam was the only member of his family who had never set foot in the Old Country. Twentieth-century history, it seemed, had conspired to keep him from his ancestral homeland.

After the Second World War, the Cold War's Iron Curtain descended upon the continent, transforming democratic Czechoslovakia into a communist state aligned with the Soviet Bloc.

As America and the Soviet Union competed on an ideological battlefield for global dominion, an artificial barrier separated Slovaks on either side of the Atlantic.

For more than four decades, the two homelands, old and new, stood on opposite sides of a deepening divide, no longer united by memory, but torn apart by politics.

The Cold War lasted forty-one long years, sundering families, breaking cultural bonds, and threatening traditions. In this tense political atmosphere, Adam came to understand that his role extended far beyond tending the family farm.

He saw himself as the custodian of the Sobota family's heritage in America. It would be Adam, not his brother or sister, who would carry the responsibility of passing down their Slovak farming traditions to future generations, with or without a bridge to Slovakia.

An Unbroken Thread
ARKANSAS, TODAY

Slovaktown is now known simply as Slovak—a name that is an eternal tribute to the origin of the town's founders.

And what became of the Sobotas? In time, Jakub and Mária took the oath and became naturalized U.S. citizens. The youngest didn't have to. Born on American soil, Adam was an American from his very first breath.

Juraj and Anna themselves never changed their allegiance. To their final days, they remained Slovak.

Today, Arkansas is the largest rice producing area in the United States, feeding America and exporting rice to more than fifty markets worldwide. The town of Slovak is home to around eighty families. Most of the people living in Slovak are descendants of pioneering Slovaks like Juraj and Anna—immigrants who settled the land in the late 19th and early 20th centuries. Though more than 130 years have passed, the people who live in Slovak still celebrate their heritage and proudly identify as descendants of the original Slovak settlers who returned to the farm.

The Sobotas' once modest homestead has been named a Centennial Farm, a distinguished honor bestowed by the state of Arkansas in recognition of a century of continuous agricultural stewardship of the land.

The farm that began as a tiny clearing carved out of wild prairie has now been expanded into nine hundred acres of fertile rice fields. This transformation seems almost miraculous in light of those first desperate years that Juraj and Anna endured.

Today, more than a century later, the land alone is worth millions, and the rice grown on those Arkansas acres still contributes to the yearly harvest that helps feed the nation.

But for the descendants of the Sobota family, the true value of their inheritance cannot be measured in dollars.

Their surname carries the memory of something far more important: the bravery of those who dared to recast themselves in a foreign land, far away from their birthplace.

Though use of the Slovak language has faded in the town of Slovak, a handful of cherished words refuse to be translated or forgotten. *Prestaň*[23], *huncút*[24], and *papuče*[25] still roll off tongues during family holidays and gatherings. Each word a connection to a world long gone yet still present.

When do the current residents feel closest to the original founders and the generations upon generations of farmers who came before?

---

23 Stop it!
24 Rascal
25 Slippers

When they cook and share Slovak food. The aroma rising from a pot of *kapustnica*[26] does more than fill the room; it transcends time and distance, unlocking memories buried deep in the body, as if coded in the very atoms of their DNA.

In those moments, carefully wrapped *holúbky* and sweet servings of *bobálky*, rolled by practiced hands, become bridges across generations—connecting past to present, and ancestors to descendants.

The Sobota women still gather to bake *koláče* in the old farm kitchens, perfecting the recipes handed down from Anna, their grandmother.

And the Sobota men proudly uphold the family's annual *klobása*-making ritual, sharing laughter, old stories, and nods of respect to the original patriarch, grandfather Juraj.

This *klobása* tradition, born long ago in the Old Country, earned such renown locally that even fellow Arkansan Bill Clinton would make special trips to the Konecny family farm to secure a supply of the cherished homemade smoked sausages. When he became the U.S. President, he requested that his annual shipment be delivered straight to the White House.

This is how a humble Slovak culinary tradition entwined with Arkansan heritage made its mark on the United States.

---

26 Sauerkraut soup

Though the Sobota family descendants are now scattered across America, many of them faithfully return each winter to the old family farm where it all began.

And they are not alone. Each year, the community gathers for Slovak Heritage Day, when the Saints Cyril and Methodius Church and the parish hall beside it come alive with music, food, and celebration of shared roots.

With great reverence, the Sobotas assemble a shrine to their past. Faded black-and-white photographs from the farm's early days, an image of Juraj stacking prairie hay, his well-worn Bible brought from the Old Country, and fragments of Anna's *kroj*, the traditional dress she wore when she faced immigration officers at Ellis Island, are proudly displayed on their table.

Each artifact carries the weight of memory, meaning, and emotion. At the center of the table sits a small pouch: the handful of soil Juraj had wrapped in a handkerchief as a talisman for his journey to America in 1895. Incredibly, the relic continues to be passed down through the generations as a cherished piece of homeland.

Among all the descendants who love reminiscing about the past, one stands out.

Johnny Sobota, a 24-year-old with an old soul. Johnny—the grandson of Adam, the first American-born Slovak from the Sobota line—has decided to close the circle his great-grandparents left open. Johnny will be the first in his family to return to the ancestral homeland.

Of course, the Slovakia that awaits Johnny is not the same place that Juraj and Anna left behind. Though the

Iron Curtain has long since rusted away, its ghosts still linger in the American imagination. Many would be surprised to discover that today's Slovakia is a modern, forward-looking country with sleek high-rises and a population that knows and has experienced the world beyond its national borders.

Yet, as Johnny drives across the flatlands of Arkansas, his soul wrestles with many questions.

> Will Slovaks recognize me as one of their own?
>
> Does anyone in Krivany remember the Sobotas?
>
> Are any living relatives left?
>
> Does the old *drevenica* still stand?

Johnny represents a new phenomenon in the American immigrant story. He belongs to a generation of Slovak-Americans who see the homeland not as a fading memory to be preserved but as a living connection to be forged or renewed.

Though Juraj and Anna never intended their farewell to Slovakia to be permanent, life—in its mysterious and unpredictable ways—had charted a different destiny for them. Now, through their great-grandson, their dream of returning to the Old Country will finally be realized.

And somewhere in the rolling Carpathians, an old wooden house waits in patient silence, ready to write the next chapter of the Sobota family tale. The story of return.

◆

In honor of the families who built Slovak, Arkansas. The Sobotas may be fictional, but the Konecnys, Bednars, Plafcans, Hooks, Uhirens, Saranies, and many others laid down real roots and built a lasting community shaped by hard work, resilience, and shared purpose.

◆

AFTERWORD: Waves of Hope

In 2026, the United States will mark its 250th anniversary, a story written not only by its founders but also by countless immigrants who built lives far from their ancestral homes. Among these were the Slovaks, whose courage, sacrifice, and perseverance became an inseparable part of the American saga.

During the Great Migration, a tidal wave of hope swept across Europe, carrying 60 million people toward the promise of the Americas. Among these immigrants were men, women, and children from Slovakia, a country that was on the cusp of transformation.

Between 1870 and 1920, an astonishing 750,000 Slovaks—more than a third of the total population of just 2 million—embarked on a perilous journey across the Atlantic Ocean.

Their departure left a permanent mark on the homeland. In eastern Slovakia, entire villages were left without men. Women like Anna Sobotová became the unsung heroes of this exodus, stepping into roles far beyond their traditional duties. These wives and mothers became providers, protectors, and family anchors.

The migration story wrote itself in success and failure, triumph and tragedy. Many men returned as promised, their pockets heavy with hard-earned American dollars. Others never made it home, claimed by dangerous mines or steel mills. Some lost their way in the seductive shadows of the New World—in gambling halls and taverns that devoured their dreams as readily as their dollars.

For most, America was meant to be temporary—a brief sojourn to earn the golden thousand dollars to buy land, tools, and livestock, and finally break free from the curse of the Old World poverty. The most remarkable were those who moved between worlds with ease, leaving and returning multiple times before making their final choice. History would come to call them "birds of passage."

Slovaks called the ones who returned from America *amerikáni*.

The *amerikáni* transformed the Slovak countryside. Returning with suitcases full of fashionable clothes and exotic artifacts, they dazzled their countrymen with their incredible stories of skyscrapers that pierced the heavens, bustling cities, people of all colors, and—most importantly—with their revolutionary ideas of literacy, democracy, and political freedom. The stories of the *amerikáni* were sparks that ignited a fire of social transformation, inspiring countless others to seek their own American dreams.

Out of the 60 million Europeans who crossed the Atlantic during the Great Migration, Slovaks represented, per capita, the second-largest ethnic group after the Irish, a remarkable outcome for such a small nation.

Yet, of the 750,000 Slovaks who left, only a third ever returned home. The rest laid the foundation for a vibrant Slovak-American community that now spans generations and numbers in the millions.

Here are some key moments in Slovak-American history:

1. Between 1870 and 1914, an astonishing 750,000 Slovaks left their homeland for America. It was an incredible one-third of the Slovak nation.

2. Many Slovaks made multiple voyages, earning them the moniker of "birds of passage."

3. Around one-third of migrants eventually returned and settled in Slovakia, enriching the country with their capital and new ideas.

4. Most Slovak immigrants settled in the industrial cities of America's Northeast and Midwest, including Pittsburgh, Pennsylvania; Cleveland, Ohio; and Chicago, Illinois. At one point, Pittsburgh, Pennsylvania, was the largest Slovak city in the world, home to a larger Slovak population than any city in Slovakia!

5. According to the 1920 US Census, approximately 620,000 Slovaks lived in the United States.

6. In the aftermath of the First World War, the United States imposed strict immigration quotas, curtailing the influx of migrants from Central and Eastern Europe. Slovaks began to settle in Canada and Argentina instead.

7. After the Second World War, Czechoslovakia became part of the Eastern Bloc. During the Cold War, the Iron Curtain created an artificial barrier, severing contact between Slovaks in America and their families in Europe for forty-one long years.

8. When the Iron Curtain came down in 1989, Slovakia reopened to the world, igniting interest on both sides of the Atlantic to rekindle lost connections

EPILOGUE: Completing the Circle

The history of Slovakia is a history of migration

No era changed Slovak society more profoundly than the Great Migration spanning the late 19th and early 20th centuries. What began as a trickle of lone men seeking fortune in America, turned into a transformative wave that altered the nation.

The men went first, creating paths that were soon taken by women, who were also eager to grasp the opportunities offered by the New World. When lone individuals became families, and families became communities, fewer emigrants looked back, and even fewer returned.

Pennsylvania, Ohio, Chicago, and New York became the new centers of Slovak life, but their influence reached as far as Connecticut, Nebraska, Arkansas, and Florida.

Wherever they went, Slovaks worked tirelessly to turn their dreams into reality. Their most enduring legacy was not calculated in dollars but in values: faith, determination, unshakable work ethic, and devotion to family. These principles, tested by hardship and strengthened by perseverance, became the foundation upon which generations of Slovak-Americans built their lives and triumphs.

Nearly 150 years after the first mass migration, much has changed, yet much remains the same.

Today, around 2 million Americans across the United States claim their Slovak heritage. These grandchildren, great-grandchildren, and great-great-grandchildren proudly carry their Slovak surnames, stories, and memories. Although most no longer speak the old language, they keep their ancestors' legacy alive in other meaningful ways through food, customs, and seasonal celebrations, with Easter and Christmas standing as powerful bridges between past and present.

More than three decades after the fall of the Iron Curtain, a new chapter is being written. Thanks to DNA testing and heritage websites, Slovak-Americans are rediscovering their roots with unprecedented enthusiasm. Proud to be American yet deeply connected to their heritage, these people have a new dream stirring in their hearts—a dream of following in the footsteps of those who came before them.

The renewed connection is strengthened by Slovakia's transformation into a modern European nation, stable and welcoming to its long-lost children.

In April 2022, the Slovak Citizenship Act was amended, allowing descendants of Slovaks up to the third generation to apply for Slovak citizenship. Slovakia now stands on the cusp of a "Great Return," ready to welcome home the great-grandchildren of those who left so long ago.

The time has come to bridge the gap between the past and the present.

Will you be the one to bring your lineage back to the land of your ancestors, where your family story began?

Here are some contemporary insights on the Slovak-America experience:

1. Nearly 2 million Americans claimed Slovak ancestry in the 1990 U.S. Census, demonstrating the enduring impact of Slovak immigration on American society and culture.
2. The 2022 amendment to Slovakia's Citizenship Act marked a historic turning point, enabling descendants up to the third generation to reclaim their Slovak citizenship—a right previously lost to their immigrant ancestors.
3. With thousands of applications currently in progress, the transformative policy promises not only to reunite families with their Slovak heritage and relatives, but also to inspire a new generation of descendants to explore opportunities to return and contribute to Slovakia's future.

ACKNOWLEDGMENTS

This book was made possible through the generosity of men and women whose requests, that reflect sharing the Slovak experience journey, an essential part of history—both in the New World and in Slovakia.

We extend a heartfelt thanks to Professor Milan Kopanic for ensuring the book's historical accuracy and to Jonathan a James Zanze and Margaret Chender for lending their valuable editorial skills.

Our deepest gratitude goes to Professor John Palka, who has believed in the mission of Global Slovakia since its very beginning. His counsel and steadfast support over the years have been truly critical in helping to share Slovakia with the world.

ACKNOWLEDGMENTS

This book was made possible through the generosity of men and women who recognize that remembering the Slovak emigration journey is an essential part of history—both in the New World and in Slovakia.

We extend a heartfelt thank you to Professor Michael Kopanic for ensuring the book's historical accuracy, and to Ken Duda, Jeanne Zulick and Margaret Bendet for lending their valuable editing skills.

Our deepest gratitude goes to Professor John Palka, who has believed in the mission of Global Slovakia since its very beginning. His counsel and steadfast support over the years have been instrumental in helping us share Slovakia with the world.

• WALL OF GRATITUDE •

With gratitude to those who supported this book, in tribute to their ancestors and the courageous journeys of emigration they undertook.

- Alexander Kulik, in memory of the Jurcak family
- Albert Kovanis, in memory of the Kovanič family.
- Lucia Soltis, in memory of the Soltis family.
- Giorgio Kandravy, in memory of the Kandravy family.
- Stephen Chastain, in memory of the Bednárik family.
- Dr Randall Moles, in memory of Janos Petrovics.
- Timothy Andrews, in memory of the Jendruch family.
- Hon. Paul M. Kanitra, in memory of the Kanitra family.
- George Hrichak, in memory of the Hrichak family.
- In memory of the Madeja family.
- Kelli Homza Rivera, in memory of the Homza family.
- Benjamin Demko, in memory of the Demko family.
- Sharon Ferguson, in memory of John Palko.
- Patricia Mika Garrard, in memory of Michael J. Mika.
- Rebecca Plafcan Johnson, in memory of the John J. Plafcan family.
- Kara Lynn, in memory of Mária Balusik.
- Dennis Plafcan, in memory of the John Plafcan family.
- Sarah Kish, in memory of the Zrelak family.
- John Jusko, in memory of the Jusko family.
- Emily Visniar-O'Neill, in memory of the Višniar family.
- John Layton, in memory of Mary (Maria) Vrablic.
- Elizabeth Massura, in memory of the Massura family.
- Beverly Bezdek Kajaria, in memory of the Bezdek family.
- Richard Novotny, in memory of the Novotný and Luks families.
- Gary Sipkovsky, in memory of the Šipkovsky, Čmiko, Vajči and Lovas families.

ABOUT THE AUTHORS

▪ ZUZANA PALOVIC, Ph.D.

Zuzana is the daughter of Slovak immigrants. She was born in communist Czechoslovakia before her family fled across the Iron Curtain to Canada, where she was raised and educated. Though she grew up far from her homeland, Zuzana never lost touch with her roots.

She studied in the United States, where she was a tennis player and an NCAA Division I athlete, earned her master's degree at the University of Amsterdam, and went on to complete her doctorate in the United Kingdom with a focus on migration.

In 2018, Zuzana returned to Slovakia and founded Global Slovakia. She has authored and co-authored six books and played a pivotal role in the One Slovak Family initiative, which drove a historic reform of the Slovak Citizenship Act—a transformative change that, for the first time in history, opened the door for Slovak descendants around the world to reconnect with their ancestral homeland through the gift of citizenship.

ABOUT THE AUTHORS

▪ GABRIELA BEREGHAZYOVA, Ph.D.

Gabriela was born in socialist Czechoslovakia and raised in independent Slovakia, where she earned a master's degree in Cultural Studies. It was there that she first encountered the history of Slovak emigration and the stories of *amerikáni*, which sparked her lifelong interest in this legacy.

She pursued further studies at prestigious universities in the United Kingdom, where she developed her distinctive approach to researching, interpreting, and sharing Slovakia's heritage with the world.

An expert on social patterns in Slovakia and the Director of *Global Slovakia*, Gabriela co-authored five books. She is dedicated to promoting Slovakia's history and culture while helping Slovaks across the globe reconnect with their ancestral homeland.

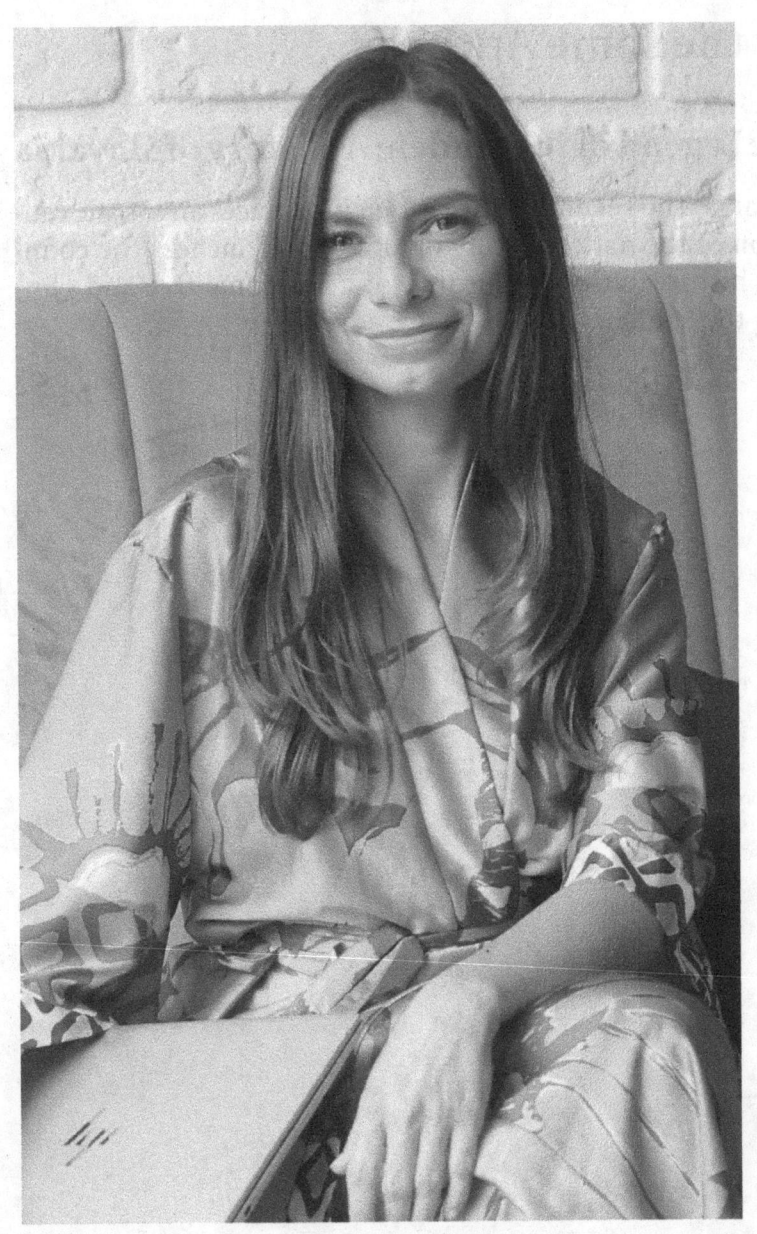

By the same Authors

The Legend of the Linden: A History of Slovakia

Slovakia: The Legend of the Linden introduces an artistic rendition of the national story of Slovakia. It anchors the country's history in the significance of its national tree and symbol—the Linden.

The Great Return

The Great Return documents the dramatic changes that took place at the beginning of the 21st century when western Europe opened its borders to the countries from behind the former Iron Curtain. Since then, more than 100 million citizens, including Slovaks, gained the freedom to move across Europe without a visa or passport. The Great Return documents the stories of those who chose to go abroad to learn and then, return to Slovakia.

Czechoslovakia: Behind the Iron Curtain

Czechoslovakia: Behind the Iron Curtain was published in 2019 to mark the 30th anniversary of the Velvet Revolution, that ended more than 40 years of communism in the country. Featuring the work of renowned documentary photographers, this book brings to life the experience of Slovaks behind the Iron Curtain.

Super Slovaks

Super Slovaks / Super Slováci is a bilingual English-Slovak book for young readers. It presents the stories of 50 Slovaks whose actions in some way benefitted their country and the world.

Slovak Settlers I., II.

Slovak Settlers invites readers to immerse themselves in the heartfelt stories of 44 Slovaks who emigrated in search of a better life. Through their voices, this book captures the emotional depth of Slovakia's migration history—shedding light on the courage, sacrifices, and resilience of those who left their homeland, and the legacy they carried across the ocean.

GLOBAL SLOVAKIA
We share Slovakia with the world

ABOUT GLOBAL SLOVAKIA

Global Slovakia is a not-for-profit non-governmental organization whose purpose is to share Slovakia with the world.

It was founded in 2017 by two Slovak scholars who are experts on their home country. Zuzana Palovic has focused on migration in Central and Eastern Europe; Gabriela Bereghazyova has focused on political and social patterns within Slovakia.

Under the leadership of Palovic and Bereghazyova, Global Slovakia has produced and published several books and has been widely represented in national and international media. The organization has also played a key role in recent changes in the Slovak Citizenship Act, giving Slovak descendants easier access to becoming Slovak citizens.

www.globalslovakia.com

- **Citizenship By Descent (CBD)**

Citizenship by Descent allows Slovak descendants abroad to reclaim their citizenship and become full members of the Slovak Republic—and the European Union. With Slovak citizenship comes the right to hold a Slovak passport, granting freedom of movement, residence, work, and study across all 27 EU member states.

Importantly, Slovak citizenship is **inheritable**. Once you secure citizenship, it automatically extends to your children, ensuring that the rights, opportunities, and protections of Slovak and EU citizenship are passed down to the next generation. This makes CBD not only a personal opportunity, but also a lasting legacy for your family.

At **Global Slovakia**, we specialize in guiding Slovak descendants through the CBD application process. We provide expert support in proving ancestry, compiling documentation, and meeting official requirements. Led by Dr. Zuzana Palovic—who played a key role in expanding Slovak citizenship eligibility—we ensure your path to citizenship is clear and achievable.

Book a 15-minute consultation today to begin your journey toward Slovak and EU citizenship at info.globalslovakia@gmail.com.

- **Slovak Living Abroad (SLA)**

The Slovak Living Abroad Certificate is official recognition of Slovak heritage for descendants living outside Slovakia. It provides practical benefits, including the right to live, study, and work in Slovakia without a special permit, simplified access to long-term residence, and opportunities to engage with Slovak cultural, social, and educational life.

At **Global Slovakia**, we support descendants in every step of the SLA application process. Our team helps you confirm eligibility, prepare documents, and navigate requirements—making it easier to reconnect with your roots and gain official recognition from Slovakia.

Book a 15-minute consultation with Dr. Zuzana Palovic to explore your eligibility for SLA citizenship at info.globalslovakia@gmail.com.

▪ Global Slovakia Academy

Global Slovakia Academy was established in 2020 by Global Slovakia to meet the growing international interest in Slovak heritage, particularly among descendants in Canada and the United States. The Academy offers 14 online programs, each designed to explore Slovakia from a unique perspective. These dynamic courses bring together valuable knowledge—often difficult to access in English—and present it in a clear, engaging, and enjoyable way.

www.globalslovakia.com

▪ Global Slovakia Webinar Series

Global Slovakia launched its webinar series in 2020. Held monthly on a donation basis, these webinars explore a wide range of themes—from Slovak history and culture to contemporary issues. Often featuring distinguished guest speakers, the series continues to grow in popularity, with our largest event attracting an international audience of more than four hundred participants.

www.globalslovakia.com

▪ Heritage Tours

Our experiences are more than tours—they are immersive journeys that create a deep and lasting connection to the land of your ancestors. And if you don't have Slovak roots, we warmly invite you to discover—and fall in love with—Slovakia.

www.globalslovakia.com

OUR PARTNERS

The National Czech & Slovak Museum & Library

NCSML engages the global community with unique Czech, Slovak, and American stories to inspire individuals with universal themes of culture, freedom, democracy, and immigration.

NCSML is an innovative leader in lifelong learning, community building, and cultural connections. We encourage self-discovery for all ages so that the stories of freedom, identity, family, and community will live on for future generations.

The NCSML was accredited by the American Alliance of Museums in November of 2008. The NCSML became a Smithsonian Affiliate in 2019.

The Office for Slovaks Living Abroad (ÚSŽZ)

ÚSŽZ carries out Slovakia's state policy toward Slovaks around the world—strengthening cultural ties, supporting education, science, and the arts, and preserving national identity. The organisation helps Slovaks stay connected to their roots while creating new opportunities for learning, creativity, and belonging.

With financial support

www.ingramcontent.com/pod-product-compliance
Lightning Source LLC
Chambersburg PA
CBHW012207090526
44583CB00022BA/2934